"The dynamic curve for most churches i[...]
has been one hundred years. Park Street [...]
has ministered effectively from the same [...]
Church historian Garth Rosell helps us see how God worked in the life of
this congregation and gives us some workable leads on why it has stayed
solid in changing cultures."

—HADDON ROBINSON
Harold John Ockenga Professor of Preaching
Gordon-Conwell Theological Seminary

"*Boston's Historic Park Street Church* is at once a wonderful read and more
than a record of the church's two hundred years of faithful ministry—it
is required reading for all who ask, 'What will ensure that my church will
be faithful to our Lord in the years that are to come?' Park Street's lesson
is this: it is extremely doubtful whether Park Street Church would still be
in existence had it not been that the heart of its message and ministry has
been sustained by emphasis on missions, periodic calls for revival and
repentance, seasons of believing prayer, and strong proclamation of Holy
Scripture on a regular basis."

—WALTER C. KAISER JR.
President Emeritus
Gordon-Conwell Theological Seminary

"For two hundred years, Park Street Church has been one of the pillars
of Christianity in North America. In this fascinating and readable
volume, master historian Garth Rosell tells the story of Park Street's
leadership in evangelicalism, missions, music and culture, education,
and social concern. Rosell's study of this Boston landmark sharpens
our understanding of the Puritan heritage, and it will inspire future
generations to keep alive the church's rich legacy."

—DANA L. ROBERT
Truman Collins Professor of World Christianity and History of Mission
Boston University School of Theology

"Seldom has a church had as enduring an impact upon the life of a nation as that of Park Street Church. Garth Rosell documents how the many educational, cultural, and social-service agencies founded under the auspices of the church have shaped the moral life of the country. *Boston's Historic Park Street Church* offers a snapshot of moral America and a timely reminder of the role played by faith-based institutions in the interests of a humane civic center."

—REV. RODNEY L. PETERSEN
Executive Director
Boston Theological Institute

"This important book is no typical congregational history. Garth Rosell has given us an exciting and inspiring story of a historic center of vital ministry that has had—and is still having—a profound impact on the hearts and minds of people around the world who are serving the cause of the gospel of Jesus Christ."

—RICHARD J. MOUW
President and Professor of Christian Philosophy
Fuller Theological Seminary

BOSTON'S HISTORIC
PARK STREET
CHURCH

BOSTON'S HISTORIC PARK STREET CHURCH

THE STORY OF AN EVANGELICAL LANDMARK

GARTH M. ROSELL

Kregel
Publications

Boston's Historic Park Street Church: The Story of an Evangelical Landmark

© 2009 by Garth M. Rosell

Published by Kregel Publications, a division of Kregel, Inc., P.O. Box 2607, Grand Rapids, MI 49501.

Cover photo: Park Street Church, Boston. Photograph by the author (2007).

Library of Congress Cataloging-in-Publication Data
Rosell, Garth.
Boston's historic Park Street Church : the story of an
    Evangelical landmark / by Garth M. Rosell.
  p. cm.
  Includes bibliographical references and index.
  1. Park Street Church (Boston, Mass.)—History. 2.
  Boston (Mass.)—Church history. I. Title.
 BX7255.B7R67 2009   285.8'74461—dc22   2008042672

ISBN 978-0-8254-3595-9

Printed in the United States of America

09 10 11 12 13 / 5 4 3 2 1

To Paul E. Toms

Beloved Pastor
Faithful Missionary
Trusted Friend

Contents

Introduction

The Rev. Dr. Gordon Hugenberger[1]

Each year about four hundred men and women, mostly in their twenties and thirties, start attending Park Street Church in Boston, Massachusetts. Despite the challenges of negotiating a large downtown church in a part of the country not known for its warm welcome, most of these newcomers manage to find their way around the church complex of four buildings, four worship services, more than fifty distinct ministries, and well over a hundred small groups. From all appearances, they soon feel at home, find needed encouragement for their faith in Christ, and become actively involved. Nevertheless, this engagement is no guarantee that they fully grasp why the church is the way it is, why it holds the distinctive convictions that it does, or how its faith, practice, and aspirations are integrally related and reflect important developments in the wider Christian church. This disconnect between active involvement and genuine understanding of the faith and practices of a particular church is all too familiar in the modern world where moves from one church to another are commonplace.

Hopefully, the ultimate explanation for the faith, practice, and

---

1. The Rev. Dr. Gordon Hugenberger has been senior minister of Park Street Church since 1997.

aspirations of Park Street Church—or of any church—is to be
found in the Word of God. It is still fair to ask, however, why certain aspects of the Christian faith are emphasized more than others, or why particular practices are followed, or why some goals are
held up and affirmed above others. The answers to these questions
require knowledge of the frequently overlooked, but fascinating
and often inspiring, history of each church.

To address this need at Park Street Church, Dr. Garth M. Rosell,
Professor of Church History at Gordon-Conwell Theological
Seminary and a member of the church, was commissioned to
write this book in honor of its Bicentennial Celebration. Rosell
is a respected authority on American church history, in particular the mid-twentieth-century revival of evangelicalism. Since the
Rev. Dr. Harold John Ockenga was senior minister of Park Street
Church from 1936 to 1969 and was a leading figure in that revival,
the choice of Rosell for this work is especially appropriate.[2]

Rosell was asked, however, to write a book that would appeal
to a much broader readership than a typical local church history,
which tries to be relatively encyclopedic in its coverage of each pastorate, major building renovation, and significant event in the life
of a church. Consequently, he was not asked to update the church
history authored forty years ago by H. Crosby Englizian, *Brimstone
Corner: Park Street Church, Boston* (Chicago: Moody Press, 1968).
Instead, Rosell was charged with two complementary tasks: select
and explicate the most significant moments in the remarkable history of Park Street Church and use these as illustrative examples to
open up to readers the broader context of some of the major developments in American church history during this two-hundred-
year period.

Congregational, Trinitarian, and Evangelical

On the signboard in front of Park Street Church are three
descriptions printed in gold lettering: Congregational, Trinitarian,

---

2. See Garth M. Rosell, *The Surprising Work of God: Harold John Ockenga, Billy
Graham, and the Rebirth of Evangelicalism* (Grand Rapids: Baker, 2008).

and Evangelical. Although these labels are worn somewhat lightly by current Park Street Church members, nevertheless they are precious and meaningful summaries of what have been the distinctive theological commitments and ideals of this church ever since its founding in 1809. To a generation that equates "new" with "improved," this continuity over two hundred years may seem surprising and, frankly, perhaps not even desirable. In almost any other organization or field of endeavor, two-hundred-year-old concepts are often mistaken or irrelevant. Indeed, given the exponential rate of scientific progress, technological advancement, societal change, and the information explosion, two hundred years may seem like an eternity.

In 1809, the year that fourteen men and twelve women founded Park Street Church, life in America was obviously very different from what it is now. Thomas Jefferson was completing his second and last term in office, and many other heroes of the American Revolution, such as Paul Revere and John and Abigail Adams, were still alive. Only fifteen states, all east of the Mississippi, had joined the Union. The population of Boston was not quite 34,000, compared to its present 591,000. The fastest mode for travel and the dissemination of information was the horse. The train would not be commercially viable until the late 1820s, and Samuel Morse (whose grandfather was among the three pastors who helped form the constituting council for Park Street Church) would not invent his electromagnetic telegraph until 1832. Cows were still being driven to the Boston Common for pasture, and only two houses on Tremont Street (then called Common Street) were more than a single story high. When the meetinghouse of Park Street Church was completed in 1810, with its 217-foot spire overtopping the State House by about 10 feet, it was the tallest building in Boston, and it remained so until 1867.

As this book makes clear, however, it is crucial to recognize that despite the outward differences between the Boston of 1809 and the present, the moral and spiritual challenges faced by our forebears two hundred years ago, and through the intervening years, are often strikingly similar to those we face today. Insofar as the answers they discovered are faithful to the Word of God, they are as relevant as ever. Isaiah wrote: "The grass withers and the flowers fall, but the word of our God stands forever" (Isa. 40:8). In response to anyone who thinks that those of another age have little to teach us, C. S. Lewis points out:

> Every age has its own outlook. It is specially good at seeing cer-
> tain truths and specially liable to make certain mistakes. We all,
> therefore, need the books [or, by extrapolation, the insights that
> are summarized in a book such as is now in your hands] that
> will correct the characteristic mistakes of our own period. . . .
> People were no cleverer then than they are now; they made as
> many mistakes as we. But not the *same* mistakes. They will not
> flatter us in the errors we are already committing; and their own
> errors, being now open and palpable, will not endanger us. Two
> heads are better than one, not because either is infallible, but
> because they are unlikely to go wrong in the same direction.[3]

Congregational

Given the location of Park Street Church in New England, it is not surprising that it is *Congregational*. In 1809, more than three quarters of the churches in Massachusetts were Congregational. This preponderance reflects the fact that most of the origi-nal settlers of Plymouth Colony in 1620 were the Pilgrims, who were Separatists. They believed it was necessary to separate from the Church of England, ruled as it was by the monarch and her appointed bishops, in order to be faithful to Christ. Soon after the Pilgrims, much larger waves of settlers, mostly of Puritans, came to establish the Massachusetts Bay Colony. The Separatists and Puritans had a similar theology and passion to see the Church of England be reformed or purified (hence the name "Puritans") of remaining elements of earlier Roman Catholic practices of worship and theology which seemed to depart from Scripture. Unlike the

3. C. S. Lewis, "On the Reading of Old Books," *God in the Dock: Essays on Theology and Ethics* (Grand Rapids: Eerdmans, 1970), 202.

Separatists, however, the Puritans hoped to accomplish this while remaining within the Church of England. Their physical separation from England, however, inevitably produced churches that were governed along Congregational lines.

This reality was formalized in 1648 when representatives of virtually all the churches of the Massachusetts Colony, the Plymouth Colony, New Hampshire, New Haven, and Connecticut met in Cambridge, Massachusetts, to agree on a uniform practice for all the churches. They produced and adopted the Cambridge Platform, which endorsed the Westminster Confession of Faith (1646) for matters of doctrine, but rejected its Presbyterial system of church government. Instead, the Cambridge Platform set forth decidedly Congregational principles for church government and discipline. This was adopted by the majority of the churches and was the legally recognized standard for Congregational churches until 1780. Although some of its details had become obsolete by that point, its broad principles continued to be applicable long afterward and explain some of the distinctive features of Park Street Church. At the core of those broad principles that define Congregational church government are two complementary convictions: the relative independence of local churches and their relative interdependence.[4]

Independence

First, Congregationalists believe that a legitimate church is formed whenever a group of individuals who accept the Scriptures as the Word of God and are committed to Jesus Christ as Lord and Savior associate themselves and their households in a relatively permanent way for the worship of God and the administration of the sacraments. Any such church has the right and ability, with God's help, to choose and set apart its own officers, adopt its own rules, arrange its own forms of worship, and otherwise manage its

---

4. For these two principles, see Richard S. Storrs, "Introduction," in *Congregationalists in America: A Popular History of Their Origin, Belief, Polity, Growth and Work* by Albert E. Dunning (New York: J. A. Hill & Co., 1894), viii; and Manfred Waldemar Kohl, *Congregationalism in America* (Oak Creek, WI: Congregational Press, 1977), 18.

own affairs. In other words, Christ has vested the authority of His
Church not in a hierarchy of professionals or bishops, who may live
far away, or even in one or two local clergy, but in the members of
the local congregation itself, especially as they are represented in
a group of ministers and elders whom they appoint. For this reason, most of the exhortations of the New Testament regarding the
life of a church are directed to the entire membership. In Matthew
18:17, for example, it is to the church as a whole that Christ entrusts
the ultimate responsibility for church discipline, rather than to any
subgroup. This divinely enabled self-governance may be viewed as
an application of the Reformation principle of "the priesthood of
all believers." As a result of this conviction, Congregationalists are
inherently ecumenical in the sense that they implicitly recognize as
a true church any church, whatever its denominational label, where
Jesus Christ is honored as the Head and its members are committed to the authority of the Word of God.[5]

Interdependence

Second, despite the affirmation of the relative independence of
each local church, Congregationalists also believe in their necessary
interdependence with other local churches and with the Christian
church through the ages. This principle of interdependence explains
why Congregational churches usually avoid describing themselves

---

5. This ecumenical conviction was seared into the conscience of Massachusetts
Congregationalists in the mid eighteenth century when the "Society for
the Propagation of the Gospel" was formed in England for the supposed
purpose of "Christianizing the Indians." Despite that stated intention, in
1762 there were thirty-one missionaries in New England sent by the society. It was clear to local Congregationalists that the society was seeking to
plant Episcopal churches in towns already supplied with Congregational
churches on the assumption that non-Episcopal churches were not genuine
churches of Christ. See Dunning, *Congregationalists in America*, 26.
   On the other hand, when Congregationalists from New England settled
in western New York and Ohio and crossed paths with Presbyterians from
Pennsylvania and elsewhere, they adopted a Plan of Union in 1801 and
agreed not to plant churches that would compete with existing Presbyterian
churches and vice versa. In congregations with a significant number of both
Congregationalists and Presbyterians, provision would be made for the
practices and mode of discipline preferred by each group, rather than allow
one group to dominate the other.

as "independent": they are not. Every church is bound by love to live in fellowship and communion with all other churches and to provide such help and counsel to those sister churches as may be welcome and needed. Likewise, churches are obligated to seek the help and counsel of sister churches whenever it would be useful to combine resources or to address some serious matter. In addition, Congregational churches are interdependent with the Christian church through time, for which reason Congregational churches willingly benefit from the use of historic creeds and confessions as imperfect, but useful summaries of the Scriptures, which provide the only infallible rule for faith and practice. Hence, when Park Street Church was founded, it required its members to adhere to both the Westminster Shorter Catechism and "The Confession of 1680," which was a revised form of the Westminster Confession of Faith.[6]

As an expression of its commitment to interdependence, Park Street Church often invited the help of other local churches and sought to be of help to them in turn. For example, when Park Street Church was organized in 1809, it invited a council of representatives from five area churches to confirm the need for a new church and to assist in its formation. Apart from that council's agreement that there was a compelling need for a new church, Park Street Church could not have been founded.[7] In 1815 when its first minister, the

---

6. Dunning, *Congregationalists in America*, 292. Park Street's requirement of adherence to these confessions is in keeping with the historic practice of Congregational churches since the Cambridge Platform of 1648, which required adherence to the Westminster Confession of Faith.

7. A key purpose in Edward D. Griffin's dedication sermon of January 10, 1810, was to make the case for this new church to the wider community, including Congregational churches that favored Unitarianism and did not participate in Park Street Church's formation council. The need was based on demographics (there had not been a new Congregational church in Boston in nearly seventy years despite a substantial increase in population) and also the desire, without condemning anyone else, to provide a place of worship for those who were committed to the historic "doctrines of grace" as set forth in the Westminster Confession of Faith and treasured by earlier Congregationalists. See Edward D. Griffin, *A Sermon Preached Jan. 10, 1810, at the Dedication of the Church in Park Street, Boston* (Boston, Lincoln & Edmands, 1810).

Rev. Dr. Edward D. Griffin, resigned with the church's clear agreement, a council of representatives from nine area churches was called in order to examine the reasons for this resignation and dismissal and to grant approval, which was necessary to ratify it.[8]

Perhaps Park Street Church's commitment to interdependence is most apparent in the many instances of cooperation in ministry outreach to Boston and the mission field through various "voluntary societies." For example, in 1812, Griffin participated in an ordination service at the Tabernacle Congregational Church in Salem for Adoniram Judson Jr., Samuel Newell, Samuel Nott, Gordon Hall, and Luther Rice. Sponsored by one such "voluntary society," the American Board of Commissioners for Foreign Missions, these five were the first missionaries to be sent from America to a foreign country. A substantial collection for their support was taken at Park Street Church the following week. Similarly, in 1816 Park Street Church joined with Old South Church in launching the City Mission Society (originally called the "Boston Society for the Religious and Moral Instruction of the Poor") in order to address the urgent needs of poor and disadvantaged residents of Boston. This is the oldest multiservice agency of its kind in New England and the second oldest in the country.

One of the most surprising examples of the commitment to interdependence among Congregational churches in eighteenth- and early nineteenth-century Boston was the regular and uniform practice of pulpit exchange. Every sermon prepared by a minister would be preached first in his own church and then, on subsequent

---

8. Such collaborative decisions were not merely an empty formality; there are intriguing cases where a council refused to allow a resigning pastor and his consenting congregation to dissolve their relationship. For instance, in 1881 the Rev. Samuel B. Andrews tendered his resignation from the Orthodox Congregational Church of Lanesville in Gloucester, Massachusetts, where he had served since 1875. The church evidently agreed, but following the usual practice, a council of pastors and representatives from other nearby churches was called to examine the reasons for this resignation. Surprisingly, the council refused to give its consent. Rev. Andrews and the church submitted to its decision, and he ministered at Lanesville for another year during which the church experienced a modest revival (fifteen persons joined the church on profession of faith in 1881–1882)!

Sundays, in every other Congregational church in town. As a result, a minister was rarely in his own pulpit on a Sunday morning. As attractive as this practice may sound, it had at least two regrettable effects. First, since ministers and their churches differed theologically in significant ways, this tended to foster sermons that were as inoffensive as possible and therefore doctrinally weak or ambiguous. Ministers who were committed to traditional Christian orthodoxy downplayed their views; ministers who had come to doubt such doctrines as the sovereignty of God, the deity of Christ, or the reality of eternal judgment avoided the topics or spoke very ambiguously.[9] Second, since the congregations knew that certain ministers denied one or more of these cardinal Christian doctrines and yet were welcomed in every pulpit, the unavoidable implication was that these must be less important matters over which it would be uncharitable to divide. Church members would naturally suppose that even if a visiting minister's "views were not absolutely correct, yet they were not deeply erroneous."[10]

Because the founders of Park Street Church saw how this uncritical practice of pulpit exchange had served to undermine genuine Christian faith elsewhere in Boston, they insisted that their minister promise not to exchange pulpits with any minister who denied the doctrine of the Trinity as explicated in the Westminster Confession of Faith.[11] So the ideal of interdependence was rightly limited to churches that share a common faith in Christ and allegiance to the Word of God; it need not include every church which wears the label of "Congregational."

Congregational at the Start of the Twenty-first Century

For two hundred years, Park Street Church has upheld these two principles of Congregationalism. Because the church valued its conservative theology and its relative independence from the

---

9. See William B. Sprague, *The Life and Sermons of Edward D. Griffin* (1839; repr., Edinburgh, U.K.: The Banner of Truth Trust, 1987), 1:101n.

10. Sprague, *The Life and Sermons of Edward D. Griffin*, 1:100.

11. H. Crosby Englizian, *Brimstone Corner: Park Street Church, Boston* (Chicago: Moody Press, 1968), 46.

control of a denominational hierarchy, it refused to follow the example of many other Congregational churches joining the United Church of Christ, which was formed in 1957 and is the largest of the three major Congregational denominations. Instead, since 1960 Park Street Church has been a member of a smaller, but vibrant and broadly evangelical denomination called the Conservative Congregational Christian Conference (or 4-Cs).

Similarly, there are many contemporary examples of Park Street Church's deliberate interdependence with sister churches. It is involved with national and regional church fellowships and has joined other local churches in outreach ministries to Boston. Park Street Church requires its missionaries to work under the auspices of established missions organizations and in close partnership with indigenous churches. Rather than planting "daughter churches," especially in areas already well served by other evangelical churches, Park Street Church seeks to strengthen nearby sister churches by advertising them on its Web site and urging members who live at an inconvenient distance to give prayerful consideration to transfer to a closer church to allow for more active involvement. A less public expression of interdependence was witnessed in 1997 after the Park Street Church Pulpit Search Committee had selected me as its final candidate. Before the committee could proceed, representative elders from Park Street Church met with the Elders of the Orthodox Congregational Church of Lanesville, where I was pastor, in order to pray together and come to agreement.

Park Street Church has maintained the commitment of early Congregationalism to shared leadership in the local church through a plurality of elders and ministers.[12] It has also extended this application of "the priesthood of all believers" to encourage maximum participation of its members in worship services and other programs. Its bylaws genuinely vest the spiritual leadership of the church in its Board of Elders, which includes the senior minister but

---

12. Cambridge Platform (1648) chapters 6 and 7. For the need for a plurality of elders and ministers in the local church, see Increase Mather, "A Disquisition Concerning Ecclesiastical Councils" (Boston, 1716; repr., Boston: Congregational Quarterly Reprint No. 2, 1870), 9–10.

is chaired by the moderator. Two ministers equally share most of the preaching load, and most of the ministers—as well as a number of missionaries and outside speakers—preach from time to time. In every service, elders have a significant role, whether leading the call to worship or offering a congregational prayer. Other church members minister through music, prayer, and, on occasion, drama or liturgical dance. Every baptism affords an opportunity for a personal statement of faith before the congregation, and members also commonly share ministry reports and personal testimonies.

Trinitarian

The second label on the signboard in front of Park Street Church is the term *Trinitarian*. The word *trinity*, a contraction of *tri* (meaning *three*) and *unity*, is used to refer to the one God who has revealed Himself in Scripture as Father, Son, and Holy Spirit. The term *trinity* is not actually in Scripture, but neither are many other theological terms whose concepts are thoroughly scriptural, such as *omniscient*, *omnipotent*, and *ineffable*. The real question is, Does Scripture, in fact, teach that God is triune? Clearly the settled conviction of the vast majority of Christians from ancient times to the present is that it does. Not surprisingly, the three earliest creeds of Christendom—the Apostles' Creed, the Nicene Creed, and the Athanasian Creed—are unanimous in their strong insistence on the doctrine of the Trinity. These three creeds are often called the "Ecumenical Creeds" not only because they are the most widely used, but also because they represent the consensus view of each of the major branches of Christendom: the Eastern and the Western, both Roman Catholic and Protestant.

As Rosell recounts in the following pages, a major reason for the founding of Park Street Church was the fact that by 1803, eight of the nine Congregational churches in Boston were served by ministers who no longer held the historic Trinitarian view of mainstream Christianity and of their Congregational predecessors and instead favored the new Unitarian perspective. As a crowning evidence of this remarkable shift in theology, in 1805 Henry Ware, who identified with the Unitarians, was elected as Hollis Professor of Divinity

at Harvard University.[13] The nation's first college and chief training ground for Congregational ministers was now led by those who
rejected historic Trinitarian Christianity. The founders of Park
Street Church were not concerned to reaffirm this Christian doctrine merely because it was traditional; their concern went far deeper.
Three central and precious truths were at stake in this debate.

The Trinity Points to a Faith Based on Revelation

First, if God is real and personal, rather than an impersonal force
or theory, our knowledge of Him, like our knowledge of any other
person, does not depend on our ability to infer what He must be
like from His actions, or to project based on our own psychology,
or to engage in philosophical speculation. Our knowledge of God
depends, instead, on God's ability and willingness to reveal Himself
to us. If Christian faith is based on God's revelation, both in the
written Word of God (Scripture) and in the incarnate Word of God
(Christ), then what counts is not our ability to construct a logical
argument to show that God must be triune rather than something
else, but on God's genuine self-disclosure as the triune God that He
is. In fact, as Christians have long realized, the mysterious nature of
the Trinity, far from being an embarrassing problem, is one of the
strongest arguments that the Christian faith is not just the result
of human invention or wishful thinking. The fact that the human
mind can scarcely grasp the mystery of the Trinity is perhaps its
chief mark of authenticity. As Augustine once observed, "If you can
comprehend it, it is not God."

Of course, there are many scriptural texts, such as Deuteronomy
6:4–5, that insist on the unity and individuality of God, against the
polytheistic idolatry of Israel's neighbors. Nevertheless, the Old
Testament often speaks of the Angel of the Lord in ways that identify

---

13. At the time Henry Ware had acknowledged only his firm opposition to
Calvinism, but this was correctly thought to be indicative of his prob-
able support for Unitarianism, which subsequently he openly defended.
Confirming this shift in theology at Harvard, in 1806 Samuel Webber, who
was favored by the Unitarians, was elected president of Harvard College.
In 1810, John Thornton Kirkland, a professed Unitarian, was elected as
Webber's successor by a substantial majority.

Him as God or the Lord. Unlike ordinary angels, He rightly receives worship and to see Him is to see God, yet He is also distinguished from God in that He sometimes speaks of God as "He," while at other times He uses "I." This happens, for example, in Genesis 16:7–13 and Exodus 3:2–15. This is entirely analogous to the New Testament's treatment of Jesus. Accordingly, Griffin, in his sermon at the 1810 dedication of Park Street Church's meetinghouse, affirmed with most Christians that these Old Testament theophanies were, in fact, manifestations of the preincarnate Son of God.

The New Testament leaves no doubt that Jesus claimed to be God and that His disciples ultimately acknowledged Him as such. For example, Jesus often speaks of His preexistence, as in John 17:5, "And now, Father, glorify me in your presence with the glory I had with you before the world began."[14] He said, "Anyone who has seen me has seen the Father" (John 14:9) and "I and the Father are one" (John 10:30), for which reason His enemies picked up stones to stone Him "for blasphemy, because you, a mere man, claim to be God" (John 10:33). Finally, after Jesus' resurrection, "Thomas said to him, 'My Lord and my God!'" (John 20:28).

Without denying Scripture's insistence on the unity of God, there are more than a dozen passages in the New Testament which mention the Father, the Son, and the Holy Spirit together in a way that confirms this three-fold distinction and implies their coequality and divinity. Jesus' so-called "Great Commission" in Matthew 28:19–20 is an obvious example: "Therefore go and make disciples of all nations, baptizing them in the name of the Father and of the Son and of the Holy Spirit, and teaching them to obey everything I have commanded you. And surely I am with you always, to the very end of the age."[15]

The Trinity Confirms God Is a God of Love

Second, the Trinity is important to Christians as an assurance that love is intrinsic to God's nature and that He loves us with an

---

14. See also Mark 10:45; John 6:38.
15. See also, e.g., 1 Cor. 12:3–6; 2 Cor. 13:14; Eph. 2:18; 4:4–6.

infinite love. The Apostle John writes: "Whoever does not love does not know God, because God is love" (1 John 4:8; cf. 4:16). As the great Congregational theologian Jonathan Edwards argued, based on the earlier work of Augustine, God's triune being is inextricably linked to His character as love. Love demands a relationship with another. If "God is love" even in eternity past before the creation of the world, then, Edwards argues, there must be within the being of God some personal self-distinctions that would allow God Himself to be a community of infinite love. Jesus assures us that this is so and that the Father loved the Son even before the creation of the world (John 17:24). That love, according to Jesus, is the model and basis for the Son's love for us (John 15:9). Just as the Father's love for the Son is expressed through self-giving and mutual indwelling (John 14:10–11), so also God pours out His love into our hearts (Rom. 5:5) and makes His home in our hearts by the Holy Spirit (John 14:23). He is in us and we are in him (1 John 4:15–16).

If God shows His self-giving love for us through the gift of His own presence in the Holy Spirit, presumably the Father's self-giving love for the Son, even from all eternity, was similarly expressed through mutual indwelling by the gift of the Holy Spirit. So Edwards suggests, following Augustine, since "God is love," perhaps God's Trinitarian being is necessary: the Father is the lover, the Son is the one who is loved, and the Holy Spirit is the means by which God expresses His love both to the Son and ultimately to us through self-giving and mutual indwelling. This is why, as Edwards points out based on 1 John 4:8–14, if we have God's Spirit dwelling in us, we have His love dwelling in us.[16]

Only if Jesus Christ is God can it be said with the Apostle Paul, "God demonstrates his own love for us in this: While we were still sinners, Christ died for us" (Rom. 5:8). Only if Jesus Christ is God will it be a comfort to consider the rhetorical questions, "Who shall separate us from the love of Christ? Shall trouble or hardship or persecution or famine or nakedness or danger or sword?" (Rom.

---

16. Jonathan Edwards, "An Unpublished Essay on the Trinity," in *An Unpublished Essay of Edwards on the Trinity*, by George P. Fisher (New York: Charles Scribner's Sons, 1903).

8:35) or to hear the promise of the risen Savior, "And surely I am with you always, to the very end of the age" (Matt. 28:20).

The Trinity Assures That Christ and the Spirit Are Sufficient for Salvation

Third, what is supremely important to Christians about the Trinity is that it is only because God is triune that sinners can be saved. To deny the Trinity is to deny that Jesus truly is God as well as man and that the Holy Spirit truly is God, not just a positive influence or spiritual force. To make these denials is to make impossible the salvation promised in Scripture. Only if Jesus is God in the flesh does His perfect life of obedience have the infinite value needed to secure eternal life and blessing for those He represents and to whom that righteousness is imputed by faith.[17] Only if Jesus is God in flesh does His death on the cross have the infinite value needed to pay in full the penalty for all of our sins, which are imputed by God to Christ, who died as our substitute.[18] As the Trinitarians put it at the time Park Street Church was founded, only if Jesus is God do we have an "infinite atonement."[19]

Likewise, only if the Spirit is really God do believers who have the Spirit have God personally dwelling in them and Christ making His home in their hearts, so they need not be spiritual orphans— technically alive, but bereft of the presence of the One who gave them life (Matt. 28:20; John 14:18, 23). Only if the Spirit of Christ, who is the Spirit of God, is living in us do we belong to Christ (Rom. 8:9) and are we truly able to have a personal relationship with God, to whom we can now pray, "Abba, Father" (Gal. 4:6).

---

17. See Rom. 3:21–22; 1 Cor. 1:30; 2 Cor. 5:21; and Phil. 3:9. Also see John Owen, *The Doctrine of Justification by Faith Through the Imputed Righteousness of Christ: Explained, Confirmed, and Vindicated* (1677; repr., Brandeston: T. Googh, 1823); and John Piper, *The Future of Justification: A Response to N. T. Wright* (Wheaton, IL: Crossway, 2007).
18. See Isa. 53:6; Rom. 3:21–26; 2 Cor. 5:21; and 1 Peter 2:24.
19. This frequent claim of the Trinitarians is opposed by William Ellery Channing, "Unitarian Christianity" (sermon delivered at the ordination of Rev. Jared Sparks in the First Independent Church of Baltimore on May 5, 1819), http://www.channingmc.org/channingspeech.html (accessed July 15, 2008).

Evangelical

The third label on the signboard in front of Park Street Church is the term *Evangelical*. The founders of Park Street Church wrote into their articles of faith: "We profess our decided attachment to that system of the [C]hristian religion which is distinguishingly denominated evangelical; more particularly to those doctrines which in a proper sense are styled the Doctrines of Grace."[20] The term *evangelical* is based on the Greek term *euangelion*, which simply means "gospel" or "good news." It is a word that Martin Luther used when he proclaimed the need for the Church to recover the true gospel, which, on the basis of Scripture alone, is the message of salvation by grace alone, through faith alone, in Christ alone, to the glory of God alone. In other words, the *gospel* is the good news that God has done for us and will do for us what we could never do for ourselves. Apart from His work, we are "dead in [our] transgressions and sins" (Eph. 2:1) and deeply unspiritual. "The man without the Spirit does not accept the things that come from the Spirit of God, for they are foolishness to him, and he cannot understand them, because they are spiritually discerned" (1 Cor. 2:14). As Jesus said to Nicodemus, "I tell you the truth, no one can see the kingdom of God unless he is born again" (John 3:3). But thanks to God's work for us through Jesus Christ, and His work in us through the Holy Spirit, we can be born again, have our sins forgiven, be made new creatures in Christ, and receive the gift of eternal life.

For the founders of Park Street Church, *evangelical* describes those who believe and are committed to live out and share with others the good news of Jesus Christ, especially as this is explicated by the church's confession of faith. In the mid twentieth century, the definition of *evangelical* was reshaped to respond to the hard lessons of the fundamentalist-modernist controversy that had dominated the first half of the century. Park Street Church's twelfth pastor, Harold John Ockenga, took a leading role in this revival of evangelicalism, along with Billy Graham, Carl F. H. Henry, and others. Evangelicalism, or neoevangelicalism as Ockenga called it,

---

20. Sprague, *The Life and Sermons of Edward D. Griffin*, 1:103.

shared with its earlier fundamentalist roots two defining convictions: an unswerving commitment to the centrality and exclusivity of the gospel of Jesus Christ, and confidence in the absolute authority and trustworthiness of Scripture as the Word of God and the only infallible rule for faith and practice.

The new evangelicals, however, differ from their fundamentalist brothers in four important respects. First, evangelicals seek to "major on the majors" and refuse to divide over important, but nevertheless secondary issues like church polity, baptism, eschatology, spiritual gifts, women in church leadership, and so on.[21] This is intended to prevent evangelicals from being unnecessarily strident and from isolating themselves from fellow Christians with whom they may not entirely agree. Second, evangelicals desire to avoid moralistic legalism while promoting true holiness and Christlike wholeness of character. Third, evangelicals strenuously affirm the social implications of the gospel. As Rosell notes, already in 1934, long before the modern civil rights movement, Ockenga denounced racism from the pulpit as "one of the greatest problems and sins of our country" and proclaimed our redemption in Christ as the basis for its most radical solution. In other messages he addressed issues of class, labor, management, and exploitation of the poor. Fourth and finally, evangelicals desire to avoid the anti-intellectualism and hostility toward science which at times has characterized fundamentalism and has hindered its serious cultural engagement and scriptural witness.

Conclusion

In the chapters that follow, Rosell invites the reader to catch an inspiring glimpse into why Park Street Church was founded, how it has remained true to its founding principles, and why it continues to thrive under God's exceptional blessing after two full centuries of ministry in the heart of Boston. It would be easy to think of the history of Park Street Church primarily in terms of the exceptionally

---

21. See Gordon P. Hugenberger, "Women in Church Office: Hermeneutics or Exegesis? A Survey of Approaches to 1 Tim. 2:8–15," *Journal of the Evangelical Theological Society* 35, no. 3 (1992): 341–60.

gifted ministers with which it has been blessed in the past, especially Edward D. Griffin and Harold John Ockenga, widely recognized as leading figures in the Second Great Awakening and the
mid-twentieth-century revival of evangelicalism respectively.

In reality, however, and true to the church's Congregational values, the real story of Park Street Church is the story of those fourteen men and twelve women who founded Park Street Church, and
many others like them. It is the story of Benjamin E. Bates, an indus-
trialist who taught a Sunday school class at Park Street Church and
who gave so generously to a seminary in Lewiston, Maine, which
had supported the abolitionist cause and was an important stop
on the underground railroad, that the school was renamed Bates
College. It is the story of twenty-three-year-old Henry A. L. French,
who wrote when he joined Park Street Church, "Hope I shall live
so as not to bring reproach upon the cause of Christ and mean to
do all I can to advance his Kingdom."[22] According to a plaque in
the sanctuary of Park Street Church, Lieutenant A. L. French gave
his life in the Battle of Gettysburg. It is the story of Se-Kyung (Sue)
Oh-Shklar, who developed the cardiac Troponin-I test for the early
diagnosis of a heart attack, used to save lives around the world; she
now cooks meals for the Woman's Benevolent Society. It is the story
of men, women, and children of every description whose names do
not appear in these pages, but are written in the Lamb's Book of
Life, and whose loving works done in the name of Christ will never
be forgotten: "The King will reply, 'I tell you the truth, whatever
you did for one of the least of these brothers of mine, you did for
me'" (Matt. 25:40).

---

22. I am grateful to Richard Elliott for drawing my attention to this example
    taken from the records for August 9, 1855, of the Examining Committee
    of Park Street Church, which are held in the Congregational Library, 14
    Beacon Street, Boston, MA.

chapter one

Planting the Seeds

When the American lawyer and statesman, Elias Boudinot, visited Boston in 1809, he discovered a landscape and community quite different from our own.[1] John Winthrop's visionary "city on a hill," populated by a mere handful of settlers in 1630, had by 1809 become a bustling city of nearly 34,000. Its burgeoning population, which would reach 93,000 by 1840, was already placing increased pressure on the tiny peninsula's limited space. While many found respite, as they had for decades, by moving to one or another of the villages that dotted the Massachusetts countryside, others were determined "to *make* more land by filling in the large expanses of tidal flats." Using landfill from nearly all of Boston's hills, Bostonians would eventually quadruple the city's available space.[2]

---

1. Milton Halsey Thomas, ed., *Elias Boudinot's Journey to Boston in 1809* (Princeton, NJ: Princeton University Press, 1955); and George Boyd, *Elias Boudinot: Patriot and Statesman, 1740–1825* (Westwood, CT: Greenwood Publications, 1969). For Boudinot's description of Boston in 1809, see Thomas, 79–80.
2. Nancy S. Seasholes, "Gaining Ground: Boston's Topographical Development in Maps," *Mapping Boston*, ed. Alex Krieger and David Cobb (Cambridge, MA: MIT Press, 2001), 119. For some fascinating descriptions and visual depictions of this growth, see Sam Bass Warner Jr., "A Brief History of Boston," *Mapping Boston*, 3–14; Nancy S. Seasholes and Amy Turner,

By the time of Boudinot's visit in 1809, however, these enormous landfill projects were only beginning to change the city's landscape. Spurred in part by what Sam Bass Warner Jr. has described as Boston's "second wave of economic prosperity," many of the city's leading families were becoming increasingly wealthy.[3] From its deepwater harbor, moreover, Boston's growing fleet of eight hundred merchant vessels was developing a thriving trade with partners in India, China, and many other exotic ports throughout the world.[4] With the expanding population, furthermore, a growing demand for goods and services was filling the purses of Boston's small shopkeepers and merchants and providing an expanding market for those who farmed the land and fished the sea.

With this growing prosperity came new hospitals, parks, churches, schools, and cultural institutions—including, by Boudinot's estimation, some twenty-four churches, seven schools, five banks, six insurance offices, three thousand houses, a 212-room hotel, more than a dozen public buildings, and "upwards of thirty benevolent useful and Charitable Societies."[5] "On the whole,

---

"Diagramming the Growth of Boston," *Mapping Boston*, 15–19; and Seashoables, "Gaining Ground," 119–45.

3. Warner, "A Brief History of Boston," 3–14. Warner has contended that a good way to comprehend the history of the city is to think in terms of waves of alternating growth and depression: prosperity from 1630–1740; depression from 1740–1790; prosperity from 1790–1921; depression from 1921–1960; prosperity from 1960–present. See especially pp. 5–6. What Warner called "a new merchant aristocracy," including the Cabots, the Lowells, the Higginsons, and the Jacksons, was established—leaving a legacy of civic benevolence (p. 6).

4. Some of Boston's newspapers carried regular news of marine traffic through the port of Boston. The *Boston Patriot*, for example, carried a regular and extensive "Marine Journal" feature listing all arrivals and departures, quarantines, foreign clearances, and coasting craft. See the 1809 *Boston Patriot* for Saturday, July 29; Wednesday, August 9; and Saturday, August 19, as examples. The reports normally appeared on page 3. Jefferson's embargo of 1807 does not appear to have been as effective as Congress had hoped and by 1810 most of its provisions had been lifted.

5. Although Boudinot speaks of twenty-four churches, he actually identifies only twenty-three: nine Congregational, two Episcopal, one Calvinistic (Park Street), four Baptist, two Methodist, one Quaker, one Roman Catholic, one Sandemanian, one Universalist, and one Unitarian. The public buildings he identified by name are the State House, the Court House, the Concert Hall, Faneuil Hall, two theaters, a jail, an Alms House, a Work

this is one of the most flourishing Towns in the United States," Boudinot observed, and he noted that it seemed to be in a position "to outstrip every other in the Union." Its "inhabitants seem to have established more of a National Character, than any other Town or State in the union," he continued, "and they appear to me, likely to become the chief Security of these States."[6] With many of the political uncertainties and economic burdens of the revolutionary era but a distant memory—although, to be sure, a new set of troubles was looming on the horizon in the growing tensions that helped to produce the War of 1812—many of Boston's hearty citizens believed the community's future to be as bright and welcoming as was the sixty-five-foot lighthouse on Little Brewster Island in Boston Harbor.[7]

Not everyone, of course, found early nineteenth-century Boston quite so welcoming. Boston's small population of free black people (most of whom lived either on Beacon Hill or in the North End) continued to struggle with the tasks of "finding decent housing, establishing independent supportive institutions, educating their children and ending slavery in the rest of the Nation."[8] The black Bostonians' construction in 1805 of the African Meeting House, the oldest black church building still standing in America, and their establishment in 1808 of a school to educate their children, were remarkable but costly achievements.

House, the Fish Market, the Glass House, and the Exchange Hotel. See Thomas, *Elias Boudinot's Journey*, 79–81. For Abel Bowen's depictions of these institutions, see William H. Whitmore, "Abel Bowen," in *The Bostonian Society Publications*, vol. 1, *Boston Old State House 1886–1888* (Boston: T. R. Marvin & Sons, 1888), 29–56.

6. Thomas, *Elias Boudinot's Journey*, 79–81.
7. See E. Digby Baltzell, *Puritan Boston and Quaker Philadelphia* (Boston: Beacon Press, 1982); Robert Campbell and Peter Vanderwarker, *Cityscapes of Boston: An American City Through Time* (Boston: Houghton Mifflin, 1992); and Lawrence W. Kennedy, *Planning the City upon a Hill: Boston Since 1630* (Amherst: University of Massachusetts Press, 1992).
8. The first national census of 1790 identified 18,000 inhabitants living in Boston, 761 of whom were free African Americans. The quotation is taken from the "Black Heritage Trail," a walking tour produced by the Boston African American National Historic Site, National Park Service, U.S. Department of the Interior.

Furthermore, as Warner reports, many sick and starving immigrants were arriving daily in Boston throughout this period with virtually no structures available to help them and with "disease [carrying] off children and women in extraordinary numbers." In addition, "drug addiction and family violence were commonplace," and many of Boston's growing population of urban poor were forced to live "in mean cellars and makeshift tenements of the worst kinds."[9]

Theological Controversy

As if these problems were not enough, a crisis of major proportions was emerging within Boston's religious community and the institutions that trained its leadership. At issue was the growing popularity of Unitarianism—a movement that emphasized a radical form of monotheism at the expense of the historic doctrine of the Trinity.[10] Emphasizing a belief that God is one person, the Father, rather than three persons in one, as the historic creeds and confessions of the Christian church have traditionally maintained, a growing number of Boston's Congregational churches began to adopt the new teaching.[11]

In a sense the teaching was not new at all. From the early years of the Christian church, as reflected in the famous debates in the early ecumenical councils, individuals such as Lucian of Antioch and Arius of Alexandria had maintained that since Jesus was begotten by the Father there must have been "a time when the Son was

9. Warner, "A Brief History of Boston," 6. See also Oscar Handlin, *Boston's Immigrants: 1790–1865* (Cambridge, MA: Harvard University Press, 1941).

10. For the history of Unitarianism, see Conrad Wright, *The Unitarian Controversy: Essays on American Unitarian History* (Boston: Skinner House Books, 1994); Sidney E. Ahlstrom, ed., *An American Reformation: A Documentary History of Unitarian Christianity* (Middletown, CT: Wesleyan University Press, 1985); and Conrad Wright, *The Beginnings of Unitarianism in America* (Berkeley, CA: Starr King, 1955).

11. For a discussion of Trinitarian theology, see Jaroslav Pelikan, *The Emergence of the Catholic Tradition (100–600)*, vol. 1 of *The Christian Tradition: A History of the Development of Doctrine* (Chicago: University of Chicago Press, 1974); and J. N. D. Kelly, *Early Christian Doctrines*, revised ed. (Peabody, MA: Prince Press, 2004).

not."[12] While affirming the importance of Jesus in carrying out God's mission in the world, the Arians and their many successors throughout history denied that Jesus was either coeternal with or "of the same substance" as the Father. This, many were convinced, allowed them to maintain the oneness of God while making room for the unique role of Christ's redemptive ministry.[13]

Given the difficulty that many Christians throughout history have experienced in grasping the subtle nuances of Trinitarian theology, one can understand why such views would become so popular among the general churchgoing population at the turn of the nineteenth century. The problem however, as the great theologian Augustine of Hippo had argued many years before, is that in order to take such a position one must also deny what God has revealed about Himself in both Scripture and creation. "For a Christian," Augustine wrote in an early catechism for young believers, "it is enough to believe that the cause of created things" is the "one true God, and that there is nothing that is not either himself or from him and that he is Trinity, that is, Father, the Son begotten from the Father, and is one and the same Spirit of Father and Son. By this Trinity, supremely, equally, and unchangeably good," he concluded, "all things have been created." Consequently, God could declare His creation "very good, since in all these things consists the wonderful beauty of the universe."[14]

Virtually all of the English Puritans who were responsible for establishing the Massachusetts Bay Colony in 1630—from John Cotton to Anne Bradstreet—would have shared St. Augustine's passionate commitment to Trinitarian theology. Indeed, the major theologians of Christian history (from Tertullian and Chrysostom

---

12. For a study of Arius, see Rowan Williams, *Arius: Heresy and Tradition*, rev. ed. (Grand Rapids: Eerdmans, 2001).
13. See Philip Schaff and Henry Wace, eds., *A Select Library of Nicene and Post-Nicene Fathers of the Christian Church*, 2nd series, vol. 14, *The Seven Ecumenical Councils* (Grand Rapids: Eerdmans, 1971), 1–190; and John Burnaby, ed., *Augustine: Later Works* (Philadelphia: Westminster Press, 1955).
14. Augustine of Hippo, *The Enchiridion on Faith, Hope, and Love*, trans. John E. Rotelle (New York: New City Press, 1999), 40–41.

to Aquinas and Calvin) and the major creeds and confessions of the Christian church (from the Apostles' and Nicene Creeds to the Augsburg and Westminster Confessions) have expressed their unswerving allegiance to the One God Who exists in three coequal and coeternal Persons (of precisely "the same substance"): God the Father, God the Son, and God the Holy Spirit. And they did so, of course, because of their shared conviction that it is *as Trinity* that the sovereign Lord of the Universe has revealed Himself in the two books we have been given to read: namely, the Holy Scriptures and God's glorious creation.[15]

Throughout the first century of Boston's history, from its founding until the early 1730s, Boston's churches remained over-whelmingly Trinitarian. However, with the arrival of the Great Awakening, as historians have tended to call the religious revivals of the mid eighteenth century, a deepening rift within the church had become increasingly apparent.[16] While many welcomed the revivals, of course, others found them deeply troubling. Some Boston pastors, like Charles Chauncy for example, watched the spread of religious revivals with fascination and growing alarm. Soon convinced that this new wave of "enthusiasm" could do significant damage to a more orderly and reasonable style of congregational life, the pastor of historic First Church in Boston, set out on a tour of New England to observe firsthand what was taking place. Far from allaying his fears, his travels prompted him to write a lengthy treatise titled *Seasonable Thoughts on the State of Religion in New*

---

15. See Jaroslav Pelikan, *Credo: Historical and Theological Guide to Creeds and Confessions of Faith in the Christian Tradition* (New Haven: Yale University Press, 2003); and Alister McGrath, *Theology: The Basics* (Oxford: Blackwell, 2004), 87–104.

16. For an interesting discussion of Boston's eleven Congregational churches during the years between 1710 and 1760 see George W. Harper, *A People So Favored of God: Boston's Congregational Churches and Their Pastors, 1710–1760*, 2nd ed. (Eugene, OR: Wipf & Stock, 2007). Harper examines First Church ("Old Brick"), Second Church ("Old North"), Third Church ("Old South"), Fourth Church ("Brattle Street"), Fifth Church ("New North"), Sixth Church ("New South"), Seventh Church ("New Brick"), Eighth Church ("Hollis Street"), Ninth Church ("West" or "Lynde Street"), Tenth Church ("Bennet Street") and Eleventh Church.

England. Documenting what he believed to be the "many and great Mistakes" of the revivals, *Seasonable Thoughts* established Chauncy as the leader of the "Old Lights," an emerging antirevival party within New England Congregationalism, and it provided the movement with its "first comprehensive statement of the new American rationalism."[17]

Jonathan Edwards, on the other hand, along with many of his prorevival colleagues, was convinced that "the surprising work of God" in Northampton, where Edwards was serving as pastor of the Congregational Church, and throughout the American colonies was fundamentally genuine.[18] Edwards's powerful defense of the revivals, along with his willingness to admit that there were indeed some aberrations in how they were being conducted, soon established him as the leader of the "New Lights" party, the ardently prorevival wing of colonial Congregationalism that formed the core of what historians now identify as American Evangelicalism.[19]

Other prominent Boston pastors, such as Jonathan Mayhew of West Congregational Church, joined Chauncy in distancing himself from Puritanism's "enthusiastic" tendencies. Indeed, as his biographer Charles Akers has observed, Mayhew "brazenly proclaimed his abandonment of Puritan theology in favor of a 'pure and undefiled' version of Christianity." Convinced that historic Trinitarian theology was fundamentally flawed, he began to teach the unity of God, the subordinate status of Jesus, and the essential goodness of

---

17. Alan Heimert and Perry Miller, eds., *The Great Awakening* (Indianapolis: Bobbs-Merrill, 1967), 292. For Chauncy, see Edward M. Griffin, *Old Brick: Charles Chauncy of Boston* (Minneapolis: University of Minnesota Press, 1980); and Charles Lippy, *Seasonable Revolutionary: The Mind of Charles Chauncy* (Lanham, MD: Rowman and Littlefield, 1981).
18. See Jonathan Edwards, "A Faithful Narrative of the Surprising Work of God in the Conversion of Many Hundred Souls in Northampton," in *The Great Awakening*, vol. 4, The Works of Jonathan Edwards, ed. C. C. Goen (New Haven: Yale University Press, 1972), 128–211. For Edwards, see George M. Marsden, *Jonathan Edwards: A Life* (New Haven: Yale University Press, 2003).
19. For the fascinating "debates" between Chauncy and Edwards, see Heimert and Miller, *The Great Awakening*, 183–363. For an excellent introduction to American Evangelicalism, see Douglas A. Sweeney, *The American Evangelical Story: A History of the Movement* (Grand Rapids: Baker Academic, 2005).

human nature. Salvation, he came to believe, did not come through radical transformation but could be achieved through the development of an enlightened moral character. Preaching this "gospel of the Enlightenment," Akers has suggested, Mayhew adopted and taught the kind of "Arminian theology" that was to make his ministry an "important way station between Puritanism and Unitarianism."[20]

The arguments of Chauncy and Mayhew soon attracted others to their perspective. Aaron Bancroft of Worcester, William Bentley of Salem, Thomas Barnard of Newbury, Ebenezer Gay of Hingham, and Samuel West of New Bedford were among a growing number who were proclaiming similar views from their pulpits. By the mid-1780s, in fact, historic King's Chapel in the heart of Boston had officially adopted a non-Trinitarian liturgy and by doing so had established itself as the city's first clearly Unitarian congregation.[21] Others soon followed their lead: including Federal Street Congregational Church (William Ellery Channing) and Brattle Street Church (Joseph Stevens Buckminster). Indeed, by the turn of the new century, the transformation in Boston Congregationalism had been nothing short of breathtaking! By 1809, when Elias Boudinot arrived in Boston, with the single exception of Old South, virtually every Congregational church in the city had been swept into the Unitarian camp. To make matters even more difficult for the Trinitarians, Henry Ware, a convinced Unitarian, had been officially installed in Harvard's prestigious Hollis Chair of Theology.[22]

Planting a Church

These massive changes in Boston's religious landscape, as one can readily understand, were deeply troubling to the city's evangelical Christians. As ardent prorevival Trinitarians, in the tradition

---

20. Charles W. Akers, *Called unto Liberty: A Life of Jonathan Mayhew, 1720–1766* (Cambridge, MA: Harvard University Press, 1964), 2 and the dust jacket.
21. Carl Scovel and Charles C. Forman, *Journey Toward Independence: King's Chapel's Transition to Unitarianism* (Boston: Skinner House Books, 1993).
22. Conrad Wright, "The Election of Henry Ware: Two Contemporary Accounts," *Harvard Library Bulletin* 17 (July 1969): 245–78. See also Wright, *The Unitarian Controversy*, 1–16.

of Jonathan Edwards and George Whitefield, a number of Boston's prominent citizens gathered regularly in each other's homes to pray for a revival of God's work in Boston and throughout the new nation. The group included William and Elizabeth Thurston, John and Hannah Tyler, and Josiah and Mary Bumstead, all members of Old South; William and Mary Ladd from Brattle Street Church; Joseph and Abigail Jenkins from First Church; Andrew and Martha Colhoun from West Church; and others such as the well-known merchant Elisha Ticknor. It is from the gatherings of this Religious Improvement Society, as it was known, that Park Street Church eventually emerged.[23]

People, Prayers, and Plans

These prayer gatherings, as has occurred so often through-out Christian history, helped to produce among the participants a fierce determination to join hands in the establishment of a truly "Biblical and orthodox church in Boston."[24] Their resolve was further strengthened in 1808 when Henry Kollock, pastor of the Independent Presbyterian Church in Savannah, Georgia, vis-ited Boston on a preaching mission. Kollock's powerful preaching impressed the members of the Religious Improvement Society so profoundly that they sent a delegation to ask if he might consider moving to Boston and becoming their leader. Kollock indicated that he was positively inclined to accept their offer but that he would do so only on condition that a church be formally gathered and a meetinghouse erected. Encouraged by Dr. Kollock's initial response, the members of the society established a committee to determine whether there was sufficient interest within the larger

---

23. The minutes of the Religious Improvement Society, covering the years between 1804 and 1808, can be found in "Park Street Congregational Church Records," Series 2, Church Records, Box 21, at the Congregational Library. See also Nathaniel Willis, "History of Park Street Church," a pre-sentation at the Thirty-sixth Annual Meeting of the congregation, March 7, 1845, Park Street Church archives.

24. Harold John Ockenga, "Our Historical Heritage" (sermon, Park Street Church, Boston, February 2, 1969), 4, Harold John Ockenga Papers, Ockenga Institute, Gordon-Conwell Theological Seminary, South Hamilton, Massachusetts (hereafter cited as Ockenga Papers).

Boston community in the possibility of erecting a new meetinghouse and whether there appeared to be adequate financial support
to make such a project possible. The response to the committee's
inquiries was heartening.

Consequently, the necessary subscription papers were drawn up
for the purpose of soliciting funds. However, since the members of
the Religious Improvement Society were also "determined to safe-
guard" the new congregation against what they believed "had either
robbed or marred the biblical witness of Boston's Congregational
churches," as H. Crosby Englizian has observed, "they built into
the warp and woof of the church's fabric a higher style of orthodoxy than prevailed at that time in the other churches." Central to
their strategy, as they made clear to the seventy-three individuals
who eventually signed the subscription papers, was the clear determination that the membership of the new church (rather than the
subscribers, the pew renters, or any other outside authority) would
hold the "exclusive power" to make all decisions on behalf of the
congregation—including the selection of its pastoral staff.[25]

By the middle of February, the early leaders of Park Street Church
were ready to make plans for the formal organization of the new
congregation. A committee was formed to secure land for a new
meetinghouse, to begin planning for its construction, and to draft
the church covenant and articles of faith.[26] At an additional meeting

---

25. Through the provisions of the trust deed, under which Park Street established its property title, all male members of the congregation were given
final authority in the selection of ministers and the sale of pews. Although
this practice became controversial in later years, it was established to help
guarantee that the doctrinal foundations of the church would continue in
perpetuity. Indeed, even after the church was incorporated in 1835, and
certain responsibilities were transferred to the Congregational Society, the
sole right to choose the minister, as Englizian has argued, remained with
the church body. See H. Crosby Englizian, *Brimstone Corner: Park Street
Church, Boston* (Chicago: Moody Press, 1968), 26–41. A handwritten copy
of the "Trustee Deed Authority" can be found among the records of Park
Street Church. During this era, many congregations used the rental or sale
of pews as a means of funding the church budget.

26. The committee consisted of Elisha Ticknor, William Thurston, John Tyler,
Josiah Bumstead, and Joseph Jenkins. The Articles of Faith, Covenant, and
Form of Admission can be found in *The Articles of Faith, and the Covenant,
of Park Street Church, Boston: With a List of the Members* (Boston: T. R.

of the committee, moderated by the pastor of the Congregational church in Charlestown, a date was set and invitations were issued to the five Congregational churches that they hoped would agree to be part of an ecclesiastical council, called together under the provisions of the Cambridge Platform of 1648 for the purpose of establishing the new congregation.[27] Given their deep theological convictions, as one might expect, the founders of Park Street Church also hoped that their exciting new initiative would provide the citizens of Boston with a "trinitarian, evangelical and orthodox" alternative to the emerging Unitarian hegemony.[28]

So it was, on February 27 of 1809, that Park Street Church was officially born.[29] Representing the Congregational churches of eastern Massachusetts at the gathering were the six members of the

Marvin, 1850); and in William B. Sprague, *Memoir of the Rev. Edward D. Griffin* (New York: Taylor & Dodd, 1839), 102–9.

27. Five sister churches were invited to participate in the ceremony: Old South and Federal Street churches in Boston, as well as the Congregational churches of Charlestown, Cambridge, and Dorchester. Both Boston congregations declined the invitation but the other three congregations, all of which had remained orthodox, accepted. For a discussion of the Cambridge Platform see Henry Wilder Foote, ed., *The Cambridge Platform of 1648* (Boston: Beacon Press, 1949).

28. The three terms, *Trinitarian*, *evangelical*, and *orthodox*, more than any others, have been used by Park Street Church to define the congregation's central theological commitments. The term *evangelical* means that "the congregation embraces the historic Biblical position of orthodoxy in doctrine. This is based on the authority of the Bible for faith and life." The term *orthodox* means that the church is committed to the historic creeds and confessions of Christian history, including the Apostles' Creed, the Nicene Creed, and the Westminster Confession. The term *Trinitarian* means that Park Street Church is "unequivocally" committed to "the unique Deity of Jesus Christ" and to "the personality and Deity of the Holy Spirit." Definitions are taken from "Park Street Church," a pamphlet published by the church in July of 1960, p. 16, Park Street Church archives.

29. Most of the records of Park Street Church are housed at the Congregational Library at 14 Beacon Street in Boston, Massachusetts. The collection, covering the years between 1804 and 1976, consists of 117 archival boxes and is titled "Boston, Massachusetts. Park Street Congregational Church Records, 1804–1976." Additional records are housed in the Park Street Church archives. Twenty-three archival boxes of materials, some of which cover the period from 1976 to the present, have recently been prepared for transfer to the permanent collection at the Congregational Library by Bethany Sayles Yu. For an excellent institutional history of Park Street Church, covering the years from its founding to 1968, see Englizian, *Brimstone Corner*.

ecclesiastical council: Abiel Holmes and John Walton of the First Church of Cambridge, Jedediah Morse and James Frothingham of the Congregational Church in Charlestown, and John Codman and James Baker of South Church in Dorchester. Under the guidance of Dr. Abiel Holmes of the Cambridge Church, who served as moderator for the meeting, the meeting was officially convened and the credentials of the twenty-six individuals who presented themselves as candidates for membership were examined and approved.

Those present then joined in a service of worship—including prayer, the reading of Acts 4, the singing of a hymn, and a sermon from Psalm 118:25 delivered by Dr. Morse. Following worship, the moderator invited those who had been accepted for membership to sign the church covenant and approve the articles of faith. He then "declared them to be a duly gathered church consonant with the ecclesiastical platform of Congregational churches" and led those assembled in prayer.[30]

A Place of Worship

The first order of business for the new congregation, in response to Dr. Kollock's stipulations, was to build a suitable meetinghouse. Within a month, a spectacular site had been purchased for $20,000 at the corner of Park Street and Tremont Street from its owners, the daughters of James and Hepzibah Swan. Peter Banner, the English architect and an admirer of the great Sir Christopher Wren, was secured to design and oversee the project; Solomon Willard, architect of the Bunker Hill Monument, was retained to design the wooden capitals of the steeple; and Benajah Brigham was hired to serve as chief mason.[31] "The Park Street founders planned to erect a meetinghouse that would tower over all others, both in height and in architectural beauty. Had more money been available, the building would have been even larger."[32]

---

30. See Englizian, *Brimstone Corner*, 29.
31. For Peter Banner, see Talbot F. Hamlin, "Peter Banner," in *Dictionary of American Biography*, ed. Allen Johnson (New York: Charles Scribner's Sons, 1927), 1:581.
32. Englizian, *Brimstone Corner*, 32–33.

Soon the old granary building, which had stood on the site for nearly a century and in which sails for the frigate *Constitution* had once been sewn, was dismantled and Park Street's stunning new sanctuary, with its magnificent 217-foot steeple, emerged in its

Park Street Church, Boston. Photograph by the author (2007).

place. Celebrated as "the most interesting mass of brick and mortar in America" by Henry James, the building had been completed in less than eight months.[33]

Peter Banner's lovely new building, in the very heart of Boston, more than met its founders' wishes for a place of worship that was both spacious and beautiful. Of far greater importance than the structure's utilitarian value and aesthetic beauty, however, was the theological statement that Park Street Church was intended to make to all who passed by its commodious facade. The soaring steeple, now a familiar part of Boston's skyline, was designed to become for succeeding generations a constant reminder of the presence of God in the midst of a great city—or as one pastor liked to phrase it, as "a finger pointing to God."[34] Furthermore, Park Street's "mass of brick and mortar," while admittedly pleasing to the eye, was intended primarily to symbolize the stability, longevity, and grandeur of "historic orthodoxy" as revealed in the Holy Scriptures and as reflected, albeit imperfectly, in the church's historic creeds and confessions. "Ours is a testimony of orthodoxy," wrote Park Street's twelfth pastor at the congregation's 150th anniversary, "in Boston, in New England, in the United States and throughout the world."[35]

The theological significance of Park Street's architectural design, however, was not limited to its external features. The sanctuary, in keeping with the stark simplicity of the congregation's Puritan lineage, was to be relatively plain and unadorned.[36] The visual

---

33. Henry James quoted by Harold John Ockenga, "The Foundations of Park Street Church" (sermon, February 22, 1959, on the occasion of the congregation's 150th anniversary), Ockenga Papers. The cornerstone of the church was laid on May 1, 1809, and the beautiful new meetinghouse was dedicated on January 10, 1810. See Edward Dorr Griffin, *A Sermon Preached Jan. 10, 1810, at the Dedication of the Church in Park Street, Boston* (Boston: Lincoln & Edmands, 1810).

34. Harold John Ockenga, "The Unique and Unparalleled Position of Park Street Church in Boston's Religious History" (sermon, 1939), Ockenga Papers.

35. Ockenga, "The Foundations of Park Street Church," 17. "Boston has always been as conscious of Park Street Church's Trinitarian testimony as a pedestrian on the common is conscious of its magnificent spire ever pointing toward heaven" (p. 2).

36. For an excellent introduction to Puritan worship and the architectural

center of the meetinghouse, accentuating Park Street's historic commitment to the unique and final authority of the Bible, was to be the pulpit—from which, as the founders clearly intended, the Word of God would be faithfully and powerfully proclaimed for as long as the building stood.[37] The windows of the new sanctuary, moreover, were to be of clear glass—allowing the congregation to look out over the common to celebrate the glory and grandeur of God's creation and to look out over the old granary burying grounds to reflect on the importance of preparing oneself for eternity.[38] The decorations and furnishings within the sanctuary, furthermore, were to be as plain as possible—to avoid any temptation to idolatry and to keep the focus of the congregation on the exposition and application of God's Word.[39]

As important as were the beauty and simplicity of the building, however, Park Street's founders were all aware, to borrow words from the great reformer Martin Luther, that "the true, real, right, essential church is a matter of the spirit and not of anything external."[40] The real Park Street, as one of its later pastors observed, is "a spiritual house of God" made up of "living stones." Its foundation is Christ. Its authority is the Bible. Its purity "is derived from its faithfulness to the Word and its practice of the Sacraments." Its apostolicity comes from its "direct connection with the Holy Spirit who called and anointed the apostles." Its unity grows out of its "submission to the Lord Jesus Christ." And its universality derives from the fact that it is made up of "people who are black and yellow and brown and white in skin" and drawn from scores of nations

structures that supported it, see Horton Davies, *The Worship of the American Puritans* (Morgan, PA: Soli Deo Gloria Publications, 1999), 270–96.

37. For a superb study of the centrality of preaching in New England, see Harry S. Stout, *The New England Soul: Preaching and Religious Culture in Colonial New England* (New York: Oxford University Press, 1986).
38. See Charles E. Hambrick-Stowe, *The Practice of Piety: Puritan Devotional Disciplines in Seventeenth-Century New England* (Chapel Hill: University of North Carolina Press, 1982), 197–241.
39. See Leland Ryken, *Worldly Saints: The Puritans as They Really Were* (Grand Rapids: Zondervan, 1986), 111–34.
40. See Ewald M. Plass, ed., *What Luther Says: An Anthology*, 3 vols. (St. Louis, MO: Concordia, 1959), 1:272.

"on five continents and the islands of the sea" through the preaching of its "missionaries on whose labors the sun never sets." These
"countless multitudes join with us and the assembly in heaven in
thanking God for the vision, faith, courage and consecration of
those twenty-six persons who originally formed this congregation
and erected this building and commenced this testimony on 'Jesus
Christ, the one foundation.'"[41]

In Pursuit of a Pastor

With the formal gathering of the congregation and the successful
completion of the meetinghouse, the founders naturally hoped to
be in a position to bring Dr. Kollock to Boston as their pastor. One
can only imagine their deep disappointment when, despite their
repeated efforts, he decided to turn down their call. Having lost
their primary candidate, therefore, the committee found it necessary to turn its attention to other possibilities, including Eliphalet
Nott, J. M. Mason, John Romeyn, Gardiner Spring, and Edward
Griffin. All of these candidates, however, eventually withdrew their
names from consideration.[42] Faced with this succession of polite
refusals, over the space of nearly two years, the leaders found themselves becoming increasingly concerned by their obvious inability
to attract the quality of leadership that they believed Park Street
needed.[43]

There was, however, an encouraging development. One of their
leading candidates, Edward Dorr Griffin, had actually moved
to the New England region to assume new responsibilities as

---

41. Ockenga, "The Foundations of Park Street Church," 2–3, 11–17.
42. Eliphalet Nott was President of Union College in Schenectady, New York;
J. M. Mason was pastor of the First Associate Reformed Church in New York
City; John Romeyn was pastor of the Cedar Street Presbyterian Church in
New York City; Gardiner Spring was pastor of the Brick Church in New
York City; and Edward Dorr Griffin shared pastoral responsibilities with
Dr. McWhorter at First Presbyterian Church in Newark, New Jersey.
43. Park Street's efforts to secure a pastor had actually begun at least two
years earlier with an invitation to Jedidiah Morse, then pastor of the
Congregational church in Charlestown. After Morse declined, members of
the Religious Improvement Society consulted with Timothy Dwight, president of Yale College, who provided the committee with some possibilities.

Bartlett Professor of Pulpit Eloquence at Andover Theological Seminary.[44] Established in 1808, as part of the evangelical response to Unitarianism's growing influence, Andover was already raising a new standard for Trinitarian orthodoxy throughout the region.[45] Timothy Dwight, the politically savvy president of Yale College, had immediately recognized the importance of the fledgling institution and, in the stirring address he gave at the opening of the new school, had provided nothing less than "a road map for the seminary's future," as historian Glenn Miller has phrased it.[46]

Edward Dorr Griffin, who joined the seminary faculty in 1809, also maintained his close association with Park Street Church—serving during the congregation's first two years as its "stated preacher."[47] A "*mammoth* of an orator," as Samuel Spring called him, Griffin not only provided the leaders of the church with helpful pastoral advice but he also preached regularly for the new congregation. He

---

44. William Sprague provides a fascinating analysis of the reasons for the decline of Trinitarian orthodoxy and the success of Unitarianism in his study of Griffin. "This lamentable defection," Sprague suggests, can be "traced, more than to any other cause, to the irregularities and extravagances that prevailed . . . during the revival of 1741 and 1742, in which Davenport and the others of the same stamp had so prominent an agency"—producing an "undue prejudice against religious excitement" and a "chilling formality" in one camp while producing "a state of indifference" in the other. Furthermore, Sprague argues, the "evangelical ministers of Boston" were unwilling to "renounce fellowship" with "Arian" leaders such as "Doctor Mayhew and Doctor Chauncy," who were "men of great power and commanding influence" within the city. Nor would the evangelical pastors challenge the longtime practice of regular preaching in each other's pulpits—a practice that virtually assured that the "leaven of Arminianism" would be "extensively diffused through nearly all of the churches." See Sprague, *Memoir of the Rev. Edward D. Griffin*, 98–105, esp. 102.
45. For the beginnings of Andover Theological Seminary in 1808, see Leonard Woods, *History of Andover Theological Seminary* (Boston: J. R. Osgood, 1885); and Glenn T. Miller, *Piety and Intellect: The Aims and Purposes of Ante-Bellum Theological Education* (Atlanta: Scholars Press, 1980), 47–83.
46. Miller, *Piety and Intellect*, 67. See Timothy Dwight, *A Sermon Preached at the Opening of the Theological Institution in Andover* (Boston: Farrand, Mallory, 1808). For an excellent study of Timothy Dwight, also see John R. Fitzmier, *New England's Moral Legislator: Timothy Dwight, 1752–1817* (Bloomington: Indiana University Press, 1998), esp. 70–72.
47. See minutes of the Religious Improvement Society and Nathaniel Willis, "History of Park Street Church."

had also been selected as the principal speaker for the dedication of the new meetinghouse on January 10, 1810.[48] A graduate of Yale College some twenty years earlier, Griffin is usually described as a large man, "six feet three in height and built in proportion," with a booming voice of "immense compass" that most of his listeners found "peculiarly melodious and solemn." Because of his strong convictions, some observers have added, he also seemed to have a special capacity for "always getting into trouble."[49]

Edward Dorr Griffin, first pastor of Park Street Church. Frontispiece from Edward D. Griffin, *A Series of Lectures, Delivered in Park Street Church, Boston, on Sabbath Evening* (Boston: Nathaniel Willis, 1813). Courtesy of Park Street Church.

The growing bond between Dr. Griffin and the Park Street congregation, coupled with the church's repeated efforts to convince him to join them as their senior pastor, finally prompted his decision to accept their invitation. Consequently, after having endured so many disappointments, one can easily understand the

48. Griffin, *A Sermon Preached Jan. 10, 1810*. The Rev. Dr. Samuel Spring is quoted in Englizian, *Brimstone Corner,* 44.
49. Griffin graduated from Yale College in 1790. The description is from Milton Halsey Thomas's superb notations in Thomas, *Elias Boudinot's Journey to Boston,* 65n. 129.

great delight of the congregation upon receiving his letter inform-
ing them of his acceptance of their pastoral call.[50] On July 31, 1811,
Edward Dorr Griffin was officially installed as the first in a line of
distinguished pastors who have served the Park Street congregation
over its first two centuries.[51]

Common Roots

Some weeks after his arrival in Boston, during the summer of
1809, the elderly statesman Elias Boudinot traveled to Andover to
see his old friend, Edward Griffin. The two had gotten acquainted
in New Jersey while Griffin was serving with Dr. McWhorter as
copastor of the First Presbyterian Church in Newark. Boudinot's
family home was located in nearby Princeton.

During their conversations together, as Boudinot described them
in his diary, they had occasion to discuss both the new theological seminary in Andover, then located on the campus of Phillips
Academy, and the new Park Street congregation in Boston.[52] The
"Calvinist Church," as Boudinot liked to call the Park Street congregation, "is a new and elegant Church, not yet quite finished,
opposite the Mall in Boston. Great opposition has been made to
him there, by the other Denominations," speaking of his friend
Griffin, who had preached a four-month series of sermons in that
place, "principally on account of his being a zealous Calvinist.
This has been increased by the propagation of the most gross
Calumnies and Falsehoods that have been reported concerning

---

50. Griffin's letter of acceptance is dated May 1, 1811. Griffin's outspoken style
along with a dispute over salary with the leaders of the church eventually
led to his resignation and return to New Jersey in 1815.

51. Sprague, *Memoir of the Rev. Edward D. Griffin*, 98–141. The fifteen senior
ministers of Park Street were Edward D. Griffin (1811–1815), Sereno E.
Dwight (1817–1826), Edward Beecher (1826–1830), Joel H. Linsley (1832–
1835), Silas Aiken (1837–1848), Andrew Leete Stone (1849–1866), William
H. H. Murray (1868–1874), John L. Withrow (1876–1887 and 1898–1907),
David Gregg (1887–1890), Isaac J. Lansing (1893–1897), Arcturus Z. Conrad
(1905–1937), Harold John Ockenga (1936–1969), Paul E. Toms (1969–1989),
David C. Fisher (1989–1995), and Gordon P. Hugenberger (1997–present).

52. Established in 1778, Phillips Academy was founded by two brothers, Samuel
and John, the sons of Samuel Phillips, the first pastor of the South Parish in
Andover. All three were graduates of Harvard.

him," Boudinot continued, "many of which I have industriously contradicted, from my own Knowledge. He is a sensible, learned, well read, able Divine—an excellent Preacher, but perhaps too warm and a little dogmatical in urging his particular Tenets, but which I doubt not proceeds from a thorough conviction that they are necessary to Salvation." Nevertheless, Boudinot concluded, "He will make his way good, and finally be acceptable to the Majority of the People."[53]

While he was visiting Andover, Boudinot also had opportunity to meet several members of the faculty and student body from the newly established Andover Theological Seminary. Deeply impressed by the preaching of Leonard Woods, one of the founders of the institution and its Abbot Professor of Christian Theology, Boudinot wrote in his diary that this man "promises to be a burning and shining light in the Church."[54] He was equally impressed by the students he met and was quite certain that they would all "become able Ministers of the New Testament." As to facilities, as he described them, there were two buildings providing lodging for fifty students, a dining room, a chapel or lecture room, and a library. He estimated that there were about thirty-five students in the college, along with five faculty members in the fields of natural theology, sacred literature, ecclesiastical history, Christian theology, and pulpit eloquence.[55]

Given the opposition to Unitarianism that had played such an important role in the founding of both institutions, one can readily understand why the early histories of Andover Theological Seminary and Park Street Church are so closely interwoven. Leaders such as Edward Griffin and Leonard Woods who maintained important

---

53. Thomas, *Elias Boudinot's Journey to Boston*, 65–66.
54. The appointment of Henry Ware (a Unitarian) as Hollis Professor of Divinity at Harvard in 1805 prompted Leonard Woods to launch the well-known "pamphlet war," sometimes called the "Wood 'n Ware Controversy," between the two on the merits of Calvinism as opposed to Unitarianism.
55. Thomas, *Elias Boudinot's Journey to Boston*, 69–70. The two institutions, Phillips Academy and Andover Theological Seminary, remained closely aligned until 1908 when a decline in student enrollment and other financial pressures forced the seminary to sell its buildings to Phillips Academy and affiliate itself with Harvard University.

ties with both the church and the seminary further reinforced these connections. Of perhaps even greater significance, however, was the fact that both institutions had committed themselves so clearly to the task of missionary outreach. "Andover became the missionary seminary," as Miller has reminded us, attracting a growing number of mission-minded students like Samuel Mills from Williams College and Adoniram Judson from Brown. At the very same time, Park Street Church was becoming one of America's most prominent missionary congregations.[56]

Spreading Seeds

Edward Dorr Griffin's impact upon the history of Park Street Church, to say nothing of his continuing influence at Andover, was enormous. Not only did his commanding presence provide much needed stability and encouragement during the congregation's early history but the deep passions of his life and ministry became, in a sense, the shared passions of the congregation as well.

Griffin's commitment to education, reflected in his appointment as Professor of Pulpit Eloquence at Andover and subsequently as President of Williams College, became such an integral part of congregational life that one could as easily unscramble an omelet as separate Park Street's ministry from the enormous academic community with which it is regularly engaged. It is not by accident, I suspect, that the congregation's first four pastors were all subsequently called to serve as college presidents: Griffin at Williams, Dwight at Hamilton, Beecher at Illinois, and Linsley at Marietta.[57] Park Street's ministry to faculty, students, lab technicians, and research scholars—from the earliest grades to the most esoteric graduate seminars—continues to be a central feature of congregational life and work.

Griffin's commitment to spiritual awakening, as understood and

---

56. On Andover Theological Seminary's missionary fervor, see Miller, *Piety and Intellect*, 77–79. On Griffin's deep commitment to world missions see Edward D. Griffin, *The Kingdom of Christ: A Missionary Sermon, Preached Before the General Assembly of the Presbyterian Church in Philadelphia, May 23, 1805* (Philadelphia: Aitken, 1805).
57. See Willis, "History of Park Street Church."

practiced by Jonathan Edwards and George Whitefield, had been a
part of his ministry from its beginning as well. The first sermon he
preached, in fact, following his graduation from Yale and his licen-
sure to preach by the West Association of New-Haven County, had
resulted in "a revival of great power," as Sprague described it, and
the gathering of "a church where there had not been one for more
than forty years."[58] Throughout his ministry, Griffin continued to
call his congregations to repentance and holiness of life. His journal is filled with descriptions of those who through the preaching
of the gospel had ceased "leaning on [the] broken reed" of their
own "good works" and had come to depend "on Him who came
to save the chief of sinners."[59] In this respect, the founders of Park
Street Church found in their new pastor a kindred spirit since they
themselves had been praying for years that God might touch New
England once again with a fresh season of spiritual awakening.

Griffin's commitment to personal and social holiness, the neces-
sity of applying biblical Christianity to every area of life, also
became a central feature of congregational life.[60] From its early
opposition to slavery, Park Street has a long and distinguished heritage of calling its members to put Christ's Great Commandment
into daily practice. "Why must the church be on the wrong side of
every major social issue?" one of Park Street's later pastors was once
asked by a soldier. "If the Bible-believing Christian is on the wrong
side of social problems such as war, race, class, labor, liquor, impe-
rialism, etc.," Harold John Ockenga responded, then "it is time
to get over the fence to the right side." Evangelical Christians, he
wrote, must abandon "ethical indifferentism." Indeed, "it is impossible to shut the Jesus of pity, healing, service, and human interest
from a Biblical theology. The higher morality of redemption does
not invalidate moral consistency."[61]

---

58. Sprague, *Memoir of the Rev. Edward D. Griffin*, 7–8.
59. Ibid., 50.
60. See, for example, the striking story of transformation in the life of a
    seventy-year-old man that Griffin recounts in Sprague, *Memoir of the Rev.
    Edward D. Griffin*, 41–42.
61. Harold John Ockenga, introduction to *The Uneasy Conscience of Modern Fun-
    damentalism*, by Carl F. H. Henry (Grand Rapids: Eerdmans, 1947), 13–14.

Griffin's commitment to world missions, at the very beginning
of what historian Kenneth Scott Latourette has called the "Great
Century" of missionary outreach, also became a major feature of
Park Street's life and ministry. "My brethren," Griffin observed,
"there is much for [us] to do. Though the world was made for
Christ, though all the nations of it are intended to swell his tri-
umph, yet, at this very moment, five parts out of six of that race for
whom he shed his sacred blood, are perishing in ignorance of his
Gospel, chained in miserable and degrading servitude to Satan."
How then, he asked, "can we forbear to cherish the pious wish that
he may enjoy the reward of his dying love? Do not our hearts throb
with desire to be instrumental in giving him *the heathen for his
inheritance, and the uttermost parts of the earth for his possession*?"[62]
Little wonder, with a regular diet of such powerful preaching, that
"the primary place in the church program of Park Street" has been
given throughout most of its history to the work of missions.[63] From
its role in the founding of the American Board of Commissioners
for Foreign Missions in the early nineteenth century to the annual
missions conferences that have characterized its life throughout the
twentieth century, Park Street has distinguished itself, in this respect
perhaps more than any other, as a missionary congregation.

Firmly Rooted

Griffin's commitment to biblical orthodoxy, as we have already
had occasion to observe, has also been a central feature of congregational life at Park Street. Dr. Griffin began a series of Sunday
evening lectures, later published under the title *A Series of Lectures,
Delivered in Park Street Church, Boston*, during the winter months
of 1812–1813. The focus of the lectures, which attracted remarkably
large crowds, was on those doctrines that Griffin was convinced
were the "great hinges" of the gospel—namely, total depravity,

---

62. Griffin, *The Kingdom of Christ*, 17. The "Haystack Prayer Group" at Williams
    College republished Griffin's address for distribution to students.
63. From a brochure, "Park Street Church, Boston, Mass.," used for distribu-
    tion to visitors during the mid twentieth century, p. 7, Park Street Church
    archives.

regeneration, election, and perseverance. "Using masterful apologetic, supported and saturated with hundreds of Scripture texts and laced with powerful logic and argument," the series was "perhaps the high point of his entire Boston ministry."[64] Griffin was not the last Park Street pastor to give himself to this important task, of course. Indeed, all of the congregation's fifteen pastors, across two centuries of history, have seen the maintenance of biblical orthodoxy as one of their major tasks and have sought to be faithful in opening the Holy Scriptures to all who will listen.

The history of Park Street Church is absolutely fascinating. Here is the place where the American Education Society, the Sandwich Islands Church, the Park Street Singing Society (a forerunner of the Handel and Haydn Society), the Boston chapter of the NAACP, the Animal Rescue League, the Prison Discipline Society, and the American Temperance Society were all established. It is where "America" was first sung, and one of America's first Sunday schools was organized, and the Near East Mission was launched, and William Lloyd Garrison's first antislavery address was delivered, and one of Charles Sumner's most important addresses was voiced, and gunpowder was stored, and the *Puritan Recorder* was published, and the offices of the National Association of Evangelicals were housed, and the Boston Evening School of the Bible was conducted, and one of America's oldest religious broadcasts originated. And it is from Park Street's famous pulpit that some of the world's best-known preachers have proclaimed the gospel: from Charles G. Finney, Dwight L. Moody, and Billy Sunday to J. Wilbur Chapman, John R. W. Stott, and Billy Graham. There is certainly much to interest contemporary visitors.

The beauty of its architecture; the vitality of its congregational life; the historic events with which it has been associated; the scores of organizations it has helped to launch; the celebrations it has hosted; the controversies it has precipitated; the missionary conferences it has held; the educational initiatives it has launched; the

---

64. Englizian, *Brimstone Corner*, 59. See Edward Dorr Griffin, *A Series of Lectures, Delivered in Park Street Church, Boston, on Sabbath Evening* (Boston: Nathaniel Willis, 1813).

publications it has produced; the revivals it has experienced; the acts of charity it has funded; the couples it has married; the ministers it has ordained; the music it has inspired; the hungry it has fed; and the thirsty souls to whom it has given "living water"—all of these stories, and so many more, are part of the history of this remarkable church and worthy of our attention.

To see them simply as isolated events or interesting anecdotes, however, would be to miss the great underlying themes that have sustained and energized Park Street Church throughout its past two hundred years. From its beginnings, the congregation's commitment to the authority of the Bible, to historic orthodoxy, to the transformative power of Christ's life, death, and resurrection, to missionary outreach, to social justice, to the importance of education, and to the need for spiritual awakening—these are the priorities that have given shape and direction to its congregational life and its ministry in the world. "Can you invest stones, brick, wood and mortar with sanctity?" asked Park Street's eleventh pastor at the congregation's 125th anniversary. "Is there any difference between this building and any other building in the City occupied with secular activities?" The answer to both questions, observed A. Z. Conrad, is a resounding "yes." When Park Street was dedicated in 1810, he continued, "it was given to holy purposes" as a "center in which the Name of Jesus Christ is magnified as the Lord of glory and in which Jesus Christ is proclaimed the Son of God, the Saviour of the world."[65]

Park Street, after all, is not primarily a monument, a museum, or a stop along Boston's Freedom Trail. It is nothing less than the house of God. "I think again of the twenty-six who constituted the first Congregation, who organized this Church," Conrad reflected in 1934, and then I think of the multitudes for whom this place has been the "Gateway of Heaven." That is why Park Street "has never proclaimed an uncertain Gospel. Its trumpet has never given an uncertain sound"—for we are among "those who believe in the

---

65. Arcturus Z. Conrad, *The One Hundred and Twenty-fifth Anniversary of Park Street Congregational Church, Boston, Massachusetts* (Boston: Park Street Church of Boston, 1934), 37.

finalities of the Faith, those unshakeable realities which endure through all the periods of time and through eternity." These are "foundations on which the soul can build."[66]

---

66. Ibid., 46.

c h a p t e r   t w o

Reaching the World

It was bitterly cold that February 6, 1812, as nearly fifteen hundred people made their way through the freshly fallen snow to attend a special service of ordination at Tabernacle Congregational Church in Salem. The five young men who were about to be ordained, all graduates of Andover Theological Seminary, sat together on a small wooden bench at the front of the sanctuary. The candidates, who would be remembered as America's first foreign missionaries, were Adoniram Judson (who had just married Ann Hasseltine the day before), Gordon Hall, Luther Rice, Samuel Nott, and Samuel Newell.[1] The atmosphere was "electric," charged by enormous emotion and anticipation, and "at times the entire assembly seemed moved as the trees of the wood are moved by a mighty wind."[2]

The service was opened in prayer by Edward D. Griffin, the pastor of Park Street Church in Boston. That he would be a prominent part

---

1. Andrew P. Peabody, *History of the Missions of the ABCFM* (Boston: Crosby and Nichols, 1862); American Board of Commissioners for Foreign Missions (ABCFM), *View of the Missions of the American Board of Commissioners for Foreign Missions* (Boston: Crocker & Brewster, 1823); and Gordon Hall and Samuel Newell, *The Conversion of the World* (Andover, MA: Flagg & Gould, 1818).
2. J. Herbert Kane, *A Concise History of the Christian World Mission* (Grand Rapids: Baker, 1987), 88.

Old Tabernacle, Salem, Massachusetts. Woodcut from Samuel M. Worcester, *A Memorial of the Old and New Tabernacle, Salem, Mass. 1854–1855* (Boston: Crocker & Brewster, 1855), 13. Courtesy of Tabernacle Congregational Church, Salem, Massachusetts.

of this historic event, along with colleagues such as Jedediah Morse, Gardiner Spring, and Samuel Worcester, was hardly a surprise.[3] Copies of his great missionary sermon, preached at the Presbyterian General Assembly in 1805, had been circulating for some years among missionary-minded students at colleges throughout the Northeast.[4] During their time at Williams College, for example, Gordon Hall, Luther Rice, Samuel J. Mills, James Richards, Ezra

3. For a description of the Salem church, see Samuel M. Worcester, *A Memorial of the Old and New Tabernacle, Salem, Mass. 1854–1855* (Boston: Crocker & Brewster, 1855), 13–80.

4. Edward D. Griffin, *The Kingdom of Christ: A Missionary Sermon, Preached Before the General Assembly of the Presbyterian Church in Philadelphia, May 23, 1805* (Philadelphia: Aitken, 1805).

Fisk, and John Steward had all been deeply affected by the sermon. Calling themselves the Society of the Brethren, these students met regularly for prayer and discussion in a grove of maple trees near the Williams College campus. On a summer's afternoon in 1806, as they were meeting to pray for the world, they were caught in a thunderstorm and sought refuge in a nearby haystack. It was there, near the spot now marked by a monument, that they committed themselves to foreign missionary service. Largely through their efforts, along with those of scores of graduates from other colleges who chose to continue their studies at Andover Theological Seminary, the Congregationalists of Massachusetts and Connecticut were inspired to launch America's first foreign missionary society—the

"Haystack Prayer Meeting" monument on the campus of Williams College. Photograph by the author (2006).

Ordination of America's first foreign missionaries, February 6, 1812, at Tabernacle Congregational Church, Salem, Massachusetts. Courtesy of Tabernacle Congregational Church.

American Board of Commissioners for Foreign Missions.[5] Modeled on earlier British structures such as the London Missionary Society, it was the ABCFM that authorized and oversaw the ordination service at 11:00 AM that cold February morning.

"If the Tabernacle in London is entitled to be called 'the cradle of the London Missionary Society,'" Samuel Worcester observed, "the Tabernacle in Salem is entitled to be called 'the cradle' both of the Massachusetts Missionary Society and the American Board of Commissioners for Foreign Mission." Had "that single ordination scene" on February 6, 1812, been the only gathering ever held in

---

5. A microfilm edition, including 858 microfilm reels, of the American Board of Commissioners for Foreign Missions records can be found at the Billy Graham Center Archives at Wheaton College in Illinois, collection 261. See also Joseph Tracy, *History of the American Board of Commissioners for Foreign Missions* (New York: M. W. Dodd, 1842); and Peabody, *History of the Missions of the ABCFM.*

this building, he continued, it alone would be "enough to hallow the memory of this revered and endeared old sanctuary."[6]

A few months before the United States declared war on England (the international conflict that led to the familiar Freedom Trail story of how brimstone, used in the manufacture of gunpowder, was stored in the basement of Park Street Church during the War of 1812), and only about two weeks after the service of ordination, Adoniram and Ann Hasseltine Judson, and Samuel and Harriet Atwood Newell left for British India from Derby Wharf in Salem on the *Caravan*. A few days later, on February 24, Samuel and Rosanna Nott along with Gordon Hall and Luther Rice set sail for India from Philadelphia on the *Harmony*. The passages took four months and involved enormous hardships—but they launched a movement that would eventually circle the globe.[7] "Such was the humble beginning of the American foreign missionary movement," observed missiologist Herbert Kane, a movement that within a century and a half was providing "almost 70 percent of the worldwide Protestant missionary force and about 80 percent of the finances."[8]

---

6. Worcester, *Memorial of the Old and New Tabernacle*, 33. While the ABCFM was not the first missionary society organized in America, it was the first to send Americans on foreign missionary service. The New York Missionary Society (1796), the Northern Missionary Society (1797), the Missionary Society of Connecticut (1798), the Massachusetts Missionary Society (1799), the Standing Committee on Missions of the Presbyterian Church (1802), the Missionary Society of Rhode Island (1803), the Western Missionary Society (1803), the Standing Committee on Missions of the Dutch Reformed Church (1806), and others had actually been established earlier. See Charles L. Chaney, *The Birth of Missions in America* (South Pasadena, CA: Carey Library, 1976).

7. For a fascinating discussion of the state of worldwide missionary activity in 1818, see Hall and Newell, *The Conversion of the World*.

8. Kane, *Concise History*, 87. For studies of the five who were ordained, see Courtney Anderson, *To the Golden Shore: The Life of Adoniram Judson* (Valley Forge, PA: Judson Press, 1987); Benjamin C. Meigs, "Memoir of the Rev. James Richards, American Missionary in Ceylon," *Missionary Herald* (1823): 241–47; Horatio Bardwell, *Memoir of Gordon Hall* (New York: J. Leavitt, 1834); James B. Taylor, *Memoir of Rev. Luther Rice* (Baltimore: Armstrong and Berry, 1841); Henry Clay Trumbull, *Old Time Student Volunteers* (New York: Revell, 1902); and William B. Sprague, *Annals of the American Pulpit* (New York: Robert Carter and Brothers, 1857), 2:531–42, 596–601.

Park Street Church, whose pastor was well-known as an advocate for worldwide evangelization, was actively engaged in the world missionary enterprise from its earliest years. We tend to "think of the Tabernacle at Salem as the church where the first five missionaries of the Board were ordained," observed W. E. Strong during Park Street's centennial celebrations in 1909, "but there were many times five missionaries of the American Board [were] ordained here." Park Street Church, Andover Theological Seminary, and the American Board were "born together," the "children of one mother." Indeed, Strong argued, "I suppose it is literally true that there is no church in America which stands quite so close to the American Board of Foreign Missions" as does this church—and "that there is no other spot in America more continuously and intimately associated with the life and progress of the American Board than the square feet embraced within this sanctuary."[9]

Central to these connections, Strong observed, were the prayers of God's people. The "Monthly Concert of Prayer for the conversion of the world," launched by the congregation in 1816, attracted an average of four to six hundred "prayer warriors" from the congregations of Park Street and Old South at each gathering. Held on the first Monday of each month, these missionary prayer meetings not only reinforced the congregation's growing interest in foreign missions but also became a seedbed for mission initiatives undertaken by the members of the church. It soon became apparent that the prayer meetings were also a feeder system for new missionary recruits.[10]

---

9. W. E. Strong, "Park Street Church and the American Board," in *Commemorative Exercises at the One Hundredth Anniversary of the Organization of Park Street Church, February 26–March 3, 1909*, ed. A. Z. Conrad (Boston: Park Street Centennial Committee, 1909), 177–81. This last quotation, from page 177, was a special favorite of Park Street's twelfth pastor, Harold John Ockenga.

10. The first of these "Monthly Concerts" was held on the first Monday of August in 1816. See Harold John Ockenga, "The Unique and Unparalleled Position of Park Street Church in Boston's Religious History" (sermon, 1939), 17, Ockenga Papers. For a discussion of the "Concert of Prayer" in American religious history, see Stephen J. Stein, introduction to *Apocalyptic Writings*, Works of Jonathan Edwards (New Haven: Yale University Press, 1977), 5:36–44.

By 1817, in fact, five young men—Elisha P. Swift, Allen Graves, John Nichols, Levi Parsons, and Daniel Buttrick—had presented themselves for missionary service. On September 3, 1817, at the same service in which Park Street's second pastor, Sereno Edwards Dwight, was ordained to the gospel ministry, the five missionary candidates were also ordained as missionaries to a needy world. "There are not a few," observed Lyman Beecher at their ordination, "who seem to regard the heathen as not accountable" for their "depravity" and "idolatry," or for their "immoralities" and "superstitions." Indeed, as some have argued, they are simply "the guileless children of our common father, all affectionately striving to please him, in ways, different indeed from those of Christian worship, but equally sincere and about equally well pleasing to God, and equally benign in their influence to make men happy on earth, and to prepare them for heaven." Why then, Beecher continued, should "so much exertion and expense" be undertaken "to relieve those, whose circumstances, for time and eternity, are as eligible as ours? Why should their reverence for the religion of their ancestors be weakened, and their 'elegant mythology' be stigmatized, and the gospel be thrust into its place? Is not God merciful? Let Him then take care of the heathen."

Such popular conceptions, Beecher thundered in response, certainly do not come from the Bible. Indeed, the Scriptures make it abundantly clear that every man, woman, boy, and girl on the face of the earth—whatever their language, culture, position, or class—stand as condemned sinners before a holy God. People of every nation, tribe, and tongue need "the Saviour, the bible, the sabbath, and the preaching of the gospel, for the same purpose, and in the same degree that we need them. If the gospel would be no blessing to them, it is none to us."

"My dear Brethren," he told the new missionaries, "the heathen are neither holy nor happy." They are "depraved" and they "must be born again.—They are ignorant, and must be instructed.—They are profligate, and must be reclaimed.—They are debased by their superstitions, and must be raised.—They are tortured by vain fears and useless penances, and must be relieved." Yet, "their groans, disregarded for ages, have at length reached the heavens; and the voice of the Almighty has come down from above, saying, 'Whom shall I send, and who will go for us?' and you, brethren, have answered, 'Here are we, send us.'" So on this special occasion, Beecher concluded, the men were "set apart, to carry the Bible and to preach the gospel, to the heathen. It is a great, but it is also a glorious work; and you are not alone. God is with you:—Jesus Christ is with you:—the Holy Spirit is with you" and "the hearts of all the pious are with you." The church pledged to them its substance and "prayers, day and night, for your protection, and comfort, and for the outpouring of the Holy Spirit upon the heathen, to whom you shall preach the gospel."[11]

The Sandwich Islands Mission

On October 15, 1819, three native Hawaiians, seven couples, and five children gathered at Park Street Church to officially "constitute the Sandwich Islands Church" in preparation for their imminent departure for the Pacific.[12] Interest in the Hawaiian Islands, of course, had been growing for nearly a decade, due in large measure to a young Hawaiian man named Opukahaia.[13] Samuel Mills, who had graduated from Williams College in 1809, had first met Opukahaia while he was studying theology at Yale and the recently converted Hawaiian was studying English. Mills invited his new friend—who had lost both parents in the tribal wars then sweeping the Hawaiian Islands—to his parents' farm in Torringford, Connecticut, where Opukahaia was surrounded by a loving Christian family. It was Mills's profound hope that the young Hawaiian, accompanied by some American missionaries, could return to the Pacific islands

11. Lyman Beecher, *The Bible a Code of Laws, a sermon delivered in Park Street Church, Boston, September 3, 1817* . . . (Andover, MA: Flagg & Gould, 1818), 47–51.
12. For a full report of the work of the ABCFM, including a description of the first three years of the Sandwich Islands Mission, see ABCFM, *View of the Missions*, 7–8. The quotation is taken from H. Crosby Englizian, *Brimstone Corner* (Chicago: Moody Press, 1968), 80–82.
13. Known in New England as Henry Obookiah, Opukahaia was born about 1792 and died in 1818. See Gardiner Spring, *Memoir of the Rev. Samuel J. Mills* (New York: J. Seymour, 1820), 50.

to spread the gospel. Although Opukahaia died before their dream could be realized, his inspiring story had become widely known.

Among those who had been touched by Mills's vision were those who gathered at Park Street Church that Friday evening in 1819. By the following week, they had set sail, aboard the *Thaddaeus*, on the long and difficult voyage to the Hawaiian Islands. Nearly six months later, on March 30, 1820, they arrived. The team of five "missionaries" (Hiram Bingham, Asa Thurston, William Richards, Charles Stewart, and Artemas Bishop), one "physician" (Abraham Blatchely), three "licensed preachers" (Samuel Whitney, Joseph Goodrich, and James Ely), one "superintendent of secular concerns" (Levi Chamberlain), one "printer" (Elisha Loomis), and three "native assistants" (Thomas Hopoo, John Honooree, and George Sandwich), as the 1823 ABCFM report phrased it, have experienced "more remarkable interpositions of Providence than any other mission on record. Its prospects of ultimate, if not of speedy success are most cheering. Almost all the principal men of the islands," the report concluded, along "with many of the common people, attend on the instructions of the missionaries" and "their congregations on the Sabbath consist of more than 1,000

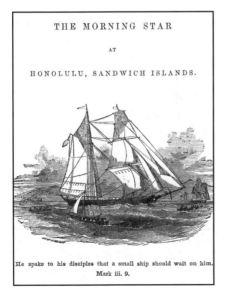

Engraving of the *Morning Star* missionary ship, April 30, 1857. Frontispiece from the "Arrival of the *Morning Star*," a twelve-page article bound with a number of other articles, tracts, and pamphlets published by the American Board of Commissioners for Foreign Missions.

persons."[14] Within two decades, the entire Bible had been translated, thousands of Hawaiians had been converted, a number of
thriving churches had been planted and more than nine hundred
schools were teaching nearly half of Hawaii's population.[15]

The remarkable success of the Sandwich Islands Mission seemed
to capture the imagination of increasing numbers of supporters
both in America and in the Pacific. On April 30, 1857, for example,
the *Commercial Advertiser* announced the arrival in the Honolulu
harbor of the beautiful new schooner, *Morning Star,* which had just
sailed to Hawaii from Boston. The ship was "no ordinary craft," as
the report phrased it, and its purposes were neither commercial nor
military. Rather, as the Honorable John Ii added in his speech of welcome, it had been purchased by the children of Hawaii and America
(more than one hundred thousand children had raised more than
$25,000—enough to purchase two of the ships—through the sale
of small amounts of "stock") solely for the purpose of carrying "the
Gospel of Jesus Christ to nations in this ocean." Since Hawaii had
been so greatly blessed by the coming of the gospel, the Hawaiian
dignitary continued, "we can afford to send it to other lands yet in
darkness. Our men and our women are going off to communicate
to others the blessings we have received. Let us not, then, tire in
this work. Let us rather increase more and more. We have received
much; let us do much."[16] The evangelized, as has so often occurred
throughout history, were becoming the evangelizers.

Given Park Street's long-standing connections with Hawaii,
one can readily understand how exciting it must have been for the
congregation when ten Hawaiian boys aged ten to fifteen, guests
of the youth department of Park Street Church, visited Boston in

---

14. See ABCFM, *View of the Missions,* 7–8.
15. See Englizian, *Brimstone Corner,* 80–83.
16. The "Address of Hon. John Ii (in Hawaiian)," and other reports of the
    arrival of the *Morning Star* were published as the final section in a collection
    of early publications of the ABCFM (various publishers) beginning with
    the *View of the Missions* report (1823) and also including the first sixteen
    "Missionary Tracts" published by the ABCFM. These were evidently bound
    together as a single volume in 1860.

December of 1958.[17] "The youngsters, equipped with earmuffs, experienced their biggest thrill when they tried ice skating for the first time," a photo of which made the front page of the *Boston Sunday Globe* for December 28, 1958. "With leis around their necks and ukuleles hanging from shoulder straps, they enthralled hundreds of onlookers at the Frog Pond on Boston Common."[18] At a festive banquet held at the church, the boys brought gifts and greetings from Dr. Paul Toms, the pastor of the thriving Haili Church in Hilo, Hawaii, and from the Fiske family, Hawaiian missionaries supported by Park Street. The missionary outreach that had been launched a century and a half earlier was still bearing fruit.

Visit of ten young Hawaiian Christians, December 1958. Photograph courtesy of Park Street Church.

---

17. The ten boys were on a "YMCA Winter Wonderland Tour" and were in Boston as guests of the Park Street Church youth department and its director, Sherwood M. Strodel.
18. Edgar W. Poore II (Park Street's business manager), undated "News Release," a copy of which can be found in the Park Street Church archives.

For the members of Park Street Church, however, the Sandwich
Islands Mission was only a beginning. By 1823, in addition to its
work in India, the American Board with the encouragement of its
friends at Park Street Church was overseeing "146 competent adult
persons, of whom more than one quarter part are preachers of the
Gospel. It has established these laborers in 25 different stations; in
six or eight different nations, speaking as many different languages,
and comprising many millions of people. It has translated a considerable part of the Bible, and is now printing it in the language
of a numerous population. It has organized 10 Christian churches
in the midst of Pagan countries; has established about 70 schools,
containing more than 3,000 scholars; and is making a gradual, but
constant and sure progress, towards raising from a degraded and
vicious barbarism, several interesting portions of our race. The
voice of the preacher is heard, and religious books and tracts are
seen to circulate, in numerous villages and the germs of Christian
civilization are beheld shooting forth in a multitude of places."[19]

Other missionary agencies, following the lead of the American
Board, soon began sending out missionaries of their own—helping
to launch what historian Kenneth Scott Latourette has called the
Great Century of missionary expansion.[20] Park Street's contribution
to this process was enormous. Within two generations, as the congregation's seventh pastor observed in 1872, 180 missionaries had
been commissioned, supported, encouraged, and sent out to spread
the gospel around the globe by the missionary-minded members of
Park Street Church.[21] The total number of missionaries supported
by the congregation throughout its history is 435, divided almost
equally between men and women. And as of 2007, about 40 percent

19. ABCFM, *View of the Missions*, 9.
20. Kenneth Scott Latourette, *A History of the Expansion of Christianity*, 7 vols.
   (Grand Rapids: Zondervan, 1970), see especially his "Great Century" vols.
   4, 5, and 6.
21. The observation by William Henry Harrison Murray, the seventh pastor
   of Park Street Church, is from Englizian, *Brimstone Corner*, 83. For the
   story of world missions, see Stephen Neill and Owen Chadwick, *A History
   of Christian Missions* (New York: Penguin, 1991); and Andrew F. Walls, *The
   Missionary Movement in Christian History* (Maryknoll, NY: Orbis, 1996).

of Park Street's annual budget was being expended for missionary outreach.[22]

Students and Women in World Missions

Much of the impetus for foreign missions during those early years and throughout the congregation's history came from students. The leadership of the older generations was essential, to be sure, but the explosive energy at the center seemed again and again to come from the missionary vision that God had planted in the hearts of younger men and women.

At scores of colleges like Williams and Brown, Middlebury and Yale, students began to gather for discussion and prayer during the early decades of the nineteenth century as they increasingly caught the vision of a needy world. Andover Theological Seminary, where many of these graduates gathered to prepare for ministry, soon became a hotbed of missionary activity. Led by Adoniram Judson and Samuel J. Mills, recent graduates from Brown and Williams, a Society of Inquiry on the Subject of Missions had been formed during Andover's early years. Not only did its members pray together regularly, they also developed strategies for advancing missionary work. Inspired by William Carey's pioneering study, *An Enquiry into the Obligations of Christians to Use Means for the Conversion of the Heathens*, they published sermons, such as Griffin's famous 1805 address, and saw to it that students read and discussed them.[23] They befriended like-minded pastors like Jedediah Morse and Samuel Worcester and faculty members like Edward Griffin and Leonard Woods, seeking "the advice, direction, and prayers of the 'Reverend Fathers,'" but also "twisting their arms" to speak out at

---

22. The figures relating to the number of missionaries are taken from a seventy-two-page listing of Park Street missionaries throughout the church's history that was provided to the writer by John Chung, Park Street's Minister of Missions. In the report, 235 were identified as female and 200 were identified as male. The budget figures are taken from the *Park Street Church 2007 Annual Report*, 2. Copies of both reports are available in the Park Street Church archives.
23. William Carey, *An Enquiry into the Obligations of Christians to Use Means for the Conversion of the Heathens* (Dallas: Criswell Publications, 1988). This influential booklet was originally published in 1792.

denominational gatherings on behalf of the missionary cause.[24] And it was largely through their efforts that organizations such as the American Board of Commissioners for Foreign Missions had finally been established.

"Every student," as an early missionary tract from the American Board phrased it, "should decide EARLY, in view of existing circumstances, whether duty requires [one] to become a missionary to the heathen."[25] Some have suggested, the author of the tract observed, "that it is better to delay deciding on [one's] personal duty to the heathen, till near the close of [one's] studies." After all, the longer one waits the more mature are the judgments, the more informed is the mind, and the more complete is the rationale. Such arguments however, the writer was convinced, seem rather to increase "the inducements to remain at home" and to harden "procrastination" into a "habit." Instead of waiting, therefore, students should seek to discover as soon as possible where God would have them spend their lives, what "field" God would wish them "to cultivate." "It is the general experience of those missionaries who came to their decision early," the article continued, that both their "courage" and their "cheer" were enriched as a result. "By long anticipation" they were "familiarized with the missionary life"—both its enormous joys and its terrible costs—and in finding their "duty" were blessed also to find "anchors to the soul." A "considerable number" of students, the article concluded, had done exactly that—swelling the ranks of foreign missionaries in the first half of the nineteenth century much as those ranks are being expanded by young men and women today.

Although the major impetus for the American missionary movement has continued to come from students, it has been the faithful labors of the Woman's Benevolent Society, more than any other single organization at Park Street Church, which has kept the missionary vision alive on the home front.[26] Established in 1809 to

---

24. See Kane, *Concise History*, 87.
25. "On Deciding Early to Become a Missionary to the Heathen," Missionary Tract, No. 7, in a collection of separate pamphlets bound together with *View of the Missions* (1823) by the ABCFM and published together in 1860.
26. From its early years, the ABCFM encouraged "the friends and patrons of

"serve God by serving others," this remarkable ministry of Park Street Church has established Sunday schools for poor children; knit socks for soldiers; raised tens of thousands of dollars for scores of good causes; sent letters and cards to the ill, shut-ins, military personnel, and missionaries; rolled bandages; prayed for students; sent CARE packages; equipped operating rooms; sponsored prayer meetings; held luncheons; cared for the needy; fed the hungry; lifted the spirits of those who were discouraged; supported the programs of the church; and done a thousand acts of quiet service besides. "There are no words to express the wonder one feels," wrote Marion P. Bruce in reflecting on the work of the society, "that so few have wrought so much."[27]

The cause of world missionary outreach has been central to the work of the Woman's Benevolent Society. Not only have the women maintained correspondence with scores of Park Street missionaries throughout the world, often providing those on the field with needed supplies, they have also taken an active role in the financial support of the missionaries who have gone out from the church. Even in the difficult years, when the cause of world missions seemed to be on the decline in the church, the society "kept the fire burning."[28] Their faithful service, in good times and bad, has been the glue that has held Park Street's missionary programs together across two centuries of the congregation's history.

"From the beginning," as missiologist Wilbert R. Shenk has pointed out, "pious women were as interested in missions as their male counterparts." Although the title "missionary" was frequently restricted during those early years to "ordained males sent to preach the gospel and found churches," Shenk argued, "from the

---

missions" to establish societies for men and women to promote the cause of world missions. For their suggested "General Plan" and "Constitution for an Auxiliary Society," see *View of the Missions*, 14–18.

27. The extensive records of this organization are in the Park Street Church archives. For the quotation and a helpful historical sketch, see Marion P. Bruce, "History of a Monument," an undated historical sketch in the Park Street archives.

28. Morton C. Campbell, sometime Treasurer of Benevolences, quoted in Bruce, "History of a Monument," 17.

beginning women were moved by the missionary call and wanted to play a full part."[29] It is too often forgotten, as Elisabeth Elliot reminded the delegates at the 1973 Urbana Missions Convention, that for many years women have "constituted the majority of foreign missionaries."[30] Not only was this true at home, as we have seen, it was true on the foreign field as well.[31]

On February 5, 1812, for example, just a day before the famous gathering for the ordination service at Tabernacle Congregational Church in Salem, Ann Hasseltine and Harriet Atwood were commissioned as "assistant missionaries."[32] Jonathan Allen, pastor of the Congregational Church in Bradford, Massachusetts, the church where Ann Hasseltine held her membership, preached the sermon. The symbolism is significant, it would seem, since it was in that very building in June of 1810 that the American Board had been established. And it was there, on this occasion, that the two women were commissioned in what historian Dana L. Robert believes may have been the first service held in America for the specific purpose of setting women apart for "a ministerial role."[33] The following day,

---

29. See Wilbert R. Shenk, general introduction to *American Women in Mission: A Social History of Their Thought and Practice,* by Dana L. Robert (Macon, GA: Mercer University Press, 1996), xii.

30. Elisabeth Elliot, "The Place of Women in World Missions," from an address delivered at the InterVarsity Urbana Conference in 1973.

31. The recovery of these stories of women missionaries is due largely to the pioneering work of gifted historians such as R. Pearce Beaver, *All Loves Excelling: American Protestant Women and World Missions* (Eugene, OR: Wipf & Stock, 1998); Dana L. Robert, ed., *Gospel Bearers, Gender Barriers* (Maryknoll, NY: Orbis, 2002); Ruth A. Tucker, *Guardians of the Great Commission: The Story of Women in Modern Missions* (Grand Rapids: Zondervan, 1988); Ruth A. Tucker and Walter Liefeld, *Daughters of the Church* (Grand Rapids: Zondervan, 1987); and William R. Hutchison, *Errand to the World: American Protestant Thought and Foreign Missions* (Chicago: University of Chicago Press, 1987).

32. For background information on these two extraordinary women, see James D. Knowles, *Memoir of Mrs. Ann H. Judson* (Boston: Lincoln & Edmands, 1831); and idem, *The Life and Writings of Mrs. Harriet Newell* (Philadelphia: American Sunday School Union, 1831).

33. Robert, *American Women in Mission,* 1. Robert points out that Leonard Woods's commission to the five men the following day was to "Go" and "preach," whereas Allen's commission to the two women was to "Go" and to "teach" (3n. 4).

February 6, Ann and Adoniram Judson traveled to Salem together to attend the ordination of America's first foreign missionaries. On that occasion, as depicted in the well-known picture (see page 58), Ann appears to be kneeling at the side of the famous bench—the hand of a sixth minister on her shoulder as the prayer of ordination is offered. Ann and Harriet, of course, were only the first of what would soon be a flood of women, both married and single, who followed the call of God to missionary service.[34] Some, like Ann and Harriet, joined hands with their husbands on scores of mission outposts around the world. Others, like the amazing pioneer single women missionaries of the Woman's Union Missionary Society, went as teachers, nurses, medical doctors, and evangelists to some of the most difficult locations on the face of the globe.[35] While the names of missionaries like William Carey, Adoniram Judson, and David Livingston might come more easily to mind than those of Eliza Gillett, Harriet Newell, and Lillian Chipley— the story of modern missions would scarcely be recognizable without them all.

Mission Strategies

While missionary outreach has remained a significant congregational priority throughout Park Street's history, three periods have been especially important in the shaping of its mission strategy.[36] The first, during the pastorate of Edward Griffin, established worldwide evangelization as a major priority for the church. The second, during the pastorate of Harold John Ockenga, launched the annual missionary conferences and established world missions as the congregation's most important financial priority. The third, during the pastorate of Gordon Hugenberger, not only developed strategies for

---

34. See Amanda Porterfield, *Mary Lyon and the Mount Holyoke Missionaries* (New York: Oxford University Press, 1997); and Robert, *American Women in Mission.*
35. For their stories see Judith MacLeod, *Woman's Union Missionary Society: The Story of a Continuing Mission* (Upper Darby, PA: InterServe USA, 1999).
36. For the missionary strategy of the early ABCFM, see Missionary Tracts, No. 1, "The Theory of Missions to the Heathen; or, the Office and Work of Foreign Missionaries" (Boston: ABCFM, n.d.).

making Park Street's missionaries a more integral part of congregational life but also began to explore ways in which the congregation
might address the new realities of a rapidly changing world both at
home and abroad.[37]

Worldwide Evangelism

One can scarcely overestimate the solid missionary foundation
established by Park Street's first pastor, Edward Griffin, and its first
generation of leaders. While they were certainly convinced that
"the Christian religion" brought with it "the blessings of education,
industry, civil liberty, family government, social order, the means
of a respectable livelihood and a well-ordered community," as the
American Board expressed it in its very first published tract, they
were equally sure that the missionary's primary calling was to be
"an ambassador for Christ"—to hold up "CHRIST AS THE ONLY
SAVIOR OF LOST SINNERS." When a "house is burning in the
dead of night," they argued, the "first and great concern is not for the
house, but for the sleeping dwellers within"—similarly, "the missionary's first and great concern is for the *soul,* to save it from impending
wrath." In due time, when men and women are truly reconciled to
God, the article continued, "a social renovation will be sure to follow." Such an approach to missionary activity, the founders argued,
remains the "good old way, marked with the footsteps of the apostles"
that brings "peace with God" and "peace with one another."[38]

Missions Conferences

In 1940, with the establishment of annual missions conferences,
Park Street entered a whole new era of missionary outreach. The congregation's "missionary interest and activity antedated the beginning of these conferences," observed Harold John Ockenga, but
they have been "radically increased through the conferences."[39]

---

37. For a fuller discussion of these changes, see Tom Telford's chapter on Park
    Street Church in *Today's All-Star Missions Churches: Strategies to Help Your
    Church Get into the Game* (Grand Rapids: Baker, 2001), 73–83.
38. ABCFM, "Theory of Missions to the Heathen," 1–22.
39. Harold John Ockenga, "What Twenty-five Years of Missionary Conferences

Harold John Ockenga, twelfth
pastor of Park Street Church.
From the Harold John Ockenga
Papers at Gordon-Conwell
Theological Seminary. Courtesy
of Gordon-Conwell Libraries.

In 1964, in a sermon looking back over twenty-five years of missions conferences at Park Street, Ockenga reflected on seven major lessons that he and the congregation had learned as a result of the gatherings. The first lesson, he was quite certain, was the discovery that "missions make the church." Park Street Church "is orthodox," he was fond of saying, but "its orthodoxy did not make the church." It "has a famous building," to be sure, but "this is not the source of its fame." It is the place where "William Lloyd Garrison gave his orations against slavery," and "Charles Sumner gave his great oration on the war system," and "'America' was first sung," and "the American Education Society, the Prison Reform Society, the Handel and Haydn Society and humanitarian movements like the Animal Rescue League" were constituted, but "it is not famous for these events." Rather, Ockenga concluded, "Park Street is known for its missionary activity." Travel "to Egypt, to Ethiopia, to Kenya, to South Africa, to the Congo, to Nigeria, to Liberia, to Ecuador, to Brazil, to Bolivia, to Mexico and to thirty or more other nations,"

Have Taught Me" (sermon, Park Street Church, Boston, 1964), Ockenga Papers.

he said, "and you will find the work of the missionaries of Park Street Church."

The second lesson was that "God has a program for His church." The program, Ockenga argued, "is outlined in [the] various forms of the Great Commission." It is "composed of (*a*) worldwide missions, (*b*) evangelism, (*c*) Christian education, and (*d*) the application of Christian truth to all realms of life. This is the program which God intends a local church to pursue. When it does, it has the assurance of divine blessing."

The third lesson, drawn from a quarter century of missions conferences, was that "the local church is the key to world missions." Although it was popular in that day as now to emphasize "the ecumenical movement, the world church, the great organizations, the merger of denominations" and the like, Ockenga observed, the Bible recognizes only two understandings of the church: "One is the local assembly in which all the life, privileges, and ministries of the church are present. The other is the universal church which is the body of Christ." Other "mediating organizations," as well-intentioned and useful as they might be, tend "to limit the missionary appeal."

The fourth lesson, growing out of the third, was that "the individual must have personal contact with the missionaries." Since "missionaries are the most wonderful people in the world," the members of Park Street would greatly enjoy and benefit from hearing them speak, entertaining them in their homes, and exchanging letters with them. Of even greater importance, however, was the congregation's need to learn from its missionaries. These individuals, Ockenga was convinced, have much to teach about the meaning of sacrifice, dedication, and worship. Many of Park Street's missionaries, he observed, are graduates "from the finest educational institutions in America." Some "could be earning enormous sums of money at home in secular professions and activities." Yet, they have given themselves to single-minded "service of the Lord."

The fifth lesson was that "the missionary conference is the most effective means of conveying the missionary challenge." Such gatherings, at which perhaps "half a hundred or more missionaries are concentrated as speakers, with appropriate exhibits and pictures," have a unique capacity to focus the attention of a congregation on the great missionary task around the world. Not only do they educate, engage, and inspire, they also call an entire community to commit its time and resources to the primary work God has called His people to do.

The sixth lesson, emerging out of the fifth, was that "the faith pledge should be used in missionary giving." The idea of making a "Faith Promise" was borrowed from the late Oswald J. Smith, longtime pastor of the People's Church in Toronto, Canada, and a frequent guest speaker in Park Street's pulpit.[40] Used for many years at Park Street, it involved "the signing of a pledge envelope" on which the person signing the envelope declared the amount of money, God helping them, that they intended to give to missions during the coming year. They may "not have the money" or even "know where the money is coming from," Ockenga explained, but they believe that God will enable them to "earn it and give it." No bill is ever sent. No reminder is ever mailed. The "pledges are between the individual and God." Yet in every one of the prior twenty-five years, Ockenga observed, "more money has come in than has been declared in the faith pledges."

The final lesson, as Ockenga concluded his reflections, was that "blessing is connected with obedience." For those who give sacrificially, there is the blessing of fellowship with God's people. For the "scores of young people" who "present themselves for service at home or abroad," there is the blessing of obedience to God's call. And for the entire congregation, insofar as it remains faithful to the Great Commission, there is the joy of knowing that "the Gospel shall be preached to every kingdom, tribe, nation and people before the end comes."[41]

Harold John Ockenga's pioneering work was continued and further strengthened by his successor, Paul E. Toms. "Since its

---

40. See Oswald J. Smith, *The Challenge of Missions* (Carlisle, PA: Paternoster, 2005), for his description of the process.
41. Ockenga, "What Twenty-five Years of Missionary Conferences Have Taught Me," 1–7.

inception," Toms observed on the fiftieth anniversary of the annual
missions conferences, Park Street has always "maintained a commitment to Missions." Under the leadership of Dr. Ockenga, however, "it took a giant step forward." Ably assisted by Betty Vetterlein,
who for nearly a quarter of a century served as director of the conferences, Park Street Church became "known around the world for
its missionary commitment."[42]

The Rev. Dr. and Mrs. Paul E. Toms. Courtesy of Park Street Church.

42. The written records of the 50th Annual Missions Conference (held in
April of 1989) can be found in the Park Street Church archives. Of Betty
Vetterlein, Dr. Toms remarked, "Her cheerful way, her devotion to detail,
and her obvious love and support of missionaries is deeply appreciated and
is honoring to our Lord."

Paul and Eva Toms had been missionaries themselves—overseeing seven churches along the Kona Coast, serving as pastor of the Haili Congregational Church in Hilo, and directing the Congregational Board of Evangelism in Australia. With their firsthand experience as missionaries, they were able to deepen the congregation's commitment to the task of world evangelization as well as to further strengthen the ties between Park Street and its own missionaries. During the years he served as pastor of Park Street Church, more than forty career missionaries left for the mission field and the church's budget for missions more than tripled. With their special interest and experience in education and world relief, moreover, Paul and Eva Toms brought to the missionary task a strong emphasis in those areas as well.[43]

A New Paradigm

While remaining deeply committed to missionary outreach both at home and abroad, Gordon Hugenberger (Park Street's fifteenth pastor) not only continued the now long-standing tradition of annual missions conferences but also sought to significantly strengthen the connections between Park Street's missionaries and the daily life and ministry of the church. In an effort "to radically strengthen the relationship between our church and our active missionaries," as he phrased it in his December 5, 1997, letter to the congregation's missionaries, the Missions Committee of Park Street Church "voted unanimously to adopt a new policy" under which any of the congregation's active missionaries could "be considered as members of our church's ministerial staff."[44] Speaking of the change as a "paradigm shift," Dr. Hugenberger went on to explain that the new policy would include the provision of "full financial support (or at least 80 percent support) for our missionaries,

---

43. For many years Dr. Toms was a member of the Board of Trustees of Gordon-Conwell Theological Seminary, serving as Chair of the Academic Affairs Committee. He has also served as President of the National Association of Evangelicals, a director of the Evangelistic Association of New England and President of World Relief, an organization that has been closely related to Park Street Church throughout its history.
44. Telford, *Missions Churches*, 76–78.

just as we would for any other member of our ministerial staff."
Missionaries who desire to be part of this new arrangement, in
return, "will consider Park Street Church to be their home church,"
will "seek to involve Park Street Church in any and all major decisions that affect their ministries," and will "normally spend their
furloughs at Park Street Church." In addition, "it is hoped that our
missionaries will take an active interest in the life of the church,
pray for its members and ministries, and cultivate close personal
relationships, as they are able, with other members of the staff
and with members of the church as a whole." The rationale for the
change in policy, as explained in the letter, was threefold: biblical
and historical precedent; proper stewardship of missionary time
and energy (especially while the missionaries are on furlough); and
the need within the church to strengthen the spiritual, emotional,
and financial support that it provides to its missionaries through
deepening friendships and more regular interaction.[45]

The proposal had been fully implemented by 1999, according to
Tom Telford, "and eight missionaries began to be fully supported by
Park Street Church. The church went from around thirty-five missionaries at 35 percent support to eight at 100 percent! By the end of
2000, there were fourteen missionaries at 100 percent support with
seventeen active missionaries and thirty-four retired missionaries
still receiving partial support."[46] By 2007, as reported in the congregation's *Annual Report*, the number of Park Street's "staff missionaries" stood at twenty-six; the number of "global professionals" was
three; and the number of the congregation's "mid-term missionaries" was six. In addition, the congregation was sponsoring short-
term missions trips, establishing "Barnabas teams," connecting
with international missions partners, actively ministering among
Boston's substantial population of international students, and
focusing attention on the city's urban community through "City

---

45. Quotations are taken from the letter of Gordon P. Hugenberger to the missionaries of Park Street Church, December 5, 1997. A copy of the letter
can be found in the Park Street Church archives and in Telford, *Missions
Churches*, 76–78.
46. Telford, *Missions Churches*, 78.

Works."[47] Although the changes, to everyone's delight, brought an immediate increase in congregational giving for world missions, they had not been implemented to make Park Street "more success-ful." Rather, as Hugenberger observed, the new paradigm had been adopted because the leaders of the congregation sincerely believed that it would better reflect "the priorities and approach of the New Testament church. If it didn't," Hugenberger added, the leaders would not have been "interested."[48]

In looking back across two centuries of ministry, it seems clear that Park Street Church has been "blessed with an exceptional heritage of sacrificial obedience to the command of Christ in support of missions." While the primary responsibility of Christians is to be ambassadors of Christ in their "homes, neighborhoods, schools, and places of employment," the church must never forget that "there are still at least 1.6 billion people on earth who live in language and culture groups where, humanly speaking, they will never hear the good news of Jesus' love from someone who exemplifies it." Consequently, it remains essential "that some Christians, whom we call missionaries, be sent out to those regions, cultures, and people groups where their presence is so desperately needed."[49]

The Challenges Ahead

The world in which we live today is vastly different from the world that surrounded Park Street Church when it was founded in 1809. Were Elias Boudinot to visit Boston again in 2009, he would surely be struck by the enormity of the changes that have taken place. Yet, I suspect he would take comfort in discovering that the primary agenda of Park Street Church has remained essentially the same. The earth may have substantially more people living on it, but their deepest needs are remarkably similar. People may have many more ways to talk with each other, but their need to communicate

---

47. *Park Street Church 2007 Annual Report*, 17. Brief reports on the various missionary programs of the church can be found in Telford, *Mission Churches*, 79–80.
48. Telford, *Missions Churches*, 81–82.
49. *Park Street Church 2001 Annual Report*, "A Self-Portrait."

remains intact. The "center of gravity" of world Christianity may have shifted to the "Global South," as Philip Jenkins and others have reminded us,[50] but the importance of world mission is as great today as it was when Boudinot's old friend, Edward Griffin, first preached his powerful missionary messages from Park Street's pulpit. While tradition can be a dead weight, when it is rooted in Scripture and brought to life by the Holy Spirit, it can also become an inspiration. For this to happen, however, as the great sixteenth-century Protestant Reformers were well aware, the church once reformed must ever be reforming—or as we might express it today, the church once renewed is in continual need of spiritual awakening.

---

50. See Philip Jenkins, *The Next Christendom: The Coming of Global Christianity* (New York: Oxford University Press, 2002).

chapter three

Awakening the Church

When the members of the Religious Improvement Society began meeting in 1804 for mutual encouragement and prayer during the formative period of Park Street's history, one of their deepest concerns was the urgent need for a fresh outpouring of God's Spirit upon Boston and throughout the world.[1] Despite their fervent prayers and Edward Griffin's deep commitment to the kind of revival that is "produced by extraordinary effusions of the divine Spirit," as Park Street's first pastor liked to express it, more than two decades were to pass before the congregation's prayers were fully answered.[2]

Not until 1822 and 1823, under the ministry of Sereno Dwight, was the congregation to experience the kind of "quiet, sane, beautiful" revival in which God transforms new believers and restores those who have drifted away. Dr. Dwight "gave himself so assiduously to the task in fervent prayer, labor and watchfulness," in fact, that the events of the revival, coupled perhaps with a case of accidental mercury poisoning, so damaged his health and depleted his

---

1. See Nathaniel Willis, "History of Park Street Church" (presentation at the Thirty-sixth Annual Meeting of the congregation, March 7, 1845), 1–3.
2. Edward D. Griffin, *A Sermon Preached Jan. 10, 1810, at the Dedication of the Church in Park Street, Boston* (Boston: Lincoln & Edmands, 1810), 26.

Sereno Edwards Dwight.
Picture at Park Street Church;
photograph by the author.

energy that "the church was compelled to give him a year's vacation in Europe and then to accept his resignation because his strength was exhausted." God seemed pleased to use his diligent efforts, however, to touch hundreds of lives and to add scores of new believers to the membership rolls of Park Street Church and its sister congregations. In 1823 alone, as Deacon Nathaniel Willis has reported, Park Street took in over one hundred new members.[3]

As the son of Timothy Dwight, the great-grandson of Jonathan Edwards, and a friend of Lyman Beecher, Sereno Edwards Dwight was no stranger to religious revivals.[4] He had seen them firsthand

3. According to Willis's report, the total number of new members added between 1809 and 1845 was 1,234 (385 men; 849 women). The largest influx of new members in any single year was 108, as a result of the revival under Dwight. The second largest influx was 102 (1842), followed by 81 (1840) and 74 (1827). See Willis, "History of Park Street Church," 3. For a listing of members each year between 1809 and 1850, see *The Articles of Faith, and the Covenant, of Park Street Church, Boston: With a List of the Members* (Boston: T. R. Marvin, 1850). The quotations are taken from Harold John Ockenga, "The Unique and Unparalleled Position of Park Street Church in Boston's Religious History" (sermon, 1939), 18, Ockenga Papers.
4. For a study of Timothy Dwight, see John R. Fitzmier, *New England's Moral Legislator: Timothy Dwight, 1752–1817* (Bloomington: Indiana University

not only during his student years at Yale College but also as a teen-ager growing up in New Haven, Connecticut, in the home of Yale's famous president.[5] Shortly after Timothy Dwight had assumed his new presidential responsibilities in 1795, he launched a counter-offensive against the forces of infidelity that he believed had taken hold on campus. Before Dwight arrived, observed Lyman Beecher, the "college was in a most ungodly state. The college church was almost extinct. Most of the students were skeptical, and rowdies were plenty. Wine and liquors were kept in many rooms," and "intemperance, profanity, gambling, and licentiousness were common."[6]

Determined to meet the challenge directly, Dwight first urged his students to build as strong a critique of "the truth of the Scriptures" as they were able to mount and as strong a defense as they could establish for their intellectual heroes, including Tom Paine, Jean-Jacques Rousseau, and Francois Marie Arouet (Voltaire). Then, in a series of powerful chapel sermons, he grappled with the issues that they had raised and he provided carefully reasoned responses. He met "ridicule with quiet argument," as J. Edwin Orr has observed. By the close of the academic year, in a memorable bac-calaureate address, he "exhorted his beloved students to 'embrace Christianity.'" Slowly but inexorably, "the tide began to turn at Yale and came in full flood in 1802. One third of the student body made profession of faith that year."[7]

Press, 1998); for Jonathan Edwards, see George M. Marsden, *Jonathan Edwards: A Life* (New Haven: Yale University Press, 2003); and for Lyman Beecher, see Stuart C. Henry, *Unvanquished Puritan: A Portrait of Lyman Beecher* (Westport, CT: Greenwood Press, 1986).

5. Sereno Edwards Dwight was the fifth son of Yale College President, Timothy Dwight. A graduate of Yale in 1803, he served as pastor of Park Street Church from 1817 until 1826 and as president of Hamilton College from 1833 until 1835.

6. Lyman Beecher, *The Autobiography of Lyman Beecher*, ed. Barbara M. Cross, 2 vols. (Cambridge, MA: Belknap Press of Harvard University Press, 1961), 1:27. Beecher was himself a Yale student at this time.

7. J. Edwin Orr, *Campus Aflame: A History of Evangelical Awakenings in Collegiate Communities* (Wheaton, IL: International Awakening Press, 1994), 40. Yale was not alone: Amherst, Dartmouth, Princeton, and Williams were among the colleges that "reported the conversion to God

Lyman Beecher, then a student at the college, was among those most deeply affected by Timothy Dwight's "polished, disciplined and logical" approach. The light "did not come in a sudden blaze," Beecher explained, "but by degrees." And throughout the process, as a guide through the darkness, there was always Dr. Dwight. "He always met me with a smile," Beecher later wrote. "Oh, how I loved him! I loved him as my own soul, and he loved me as a son." Later, during his pastoral ministry in Litchfield, Connecticut, Beecher told his old teacher that everything he had he owed to him. "Then," Dwight responded, "I have done a great and soul-satisfying work. I consider myself amply rewarded."[8] Early in 1817, having suffered for many months with "a painful form of cancer," Timothy Dwight died. "The Light of Yale is extinguished," lamented Gardiner Spring at the funeral; "The vital fire is fled." "Dr. Dwight is gone!" was Beecher's response, "My father! My father! The chariots of Israel and the horsemen thereof!"[9]

Dwight's Ordination, September 3, 1817

With the death of his father such a recent memory, one can easily understand why Sereno Dwight would have wanted his old friend Lyman Beecher to preach the sermon at his ordination. Using Psalm 19 as his text, Beecher began by describing the glory of God—reflected clearly in the magnificence of creation and in the words of Holy Scripture—and then he turned to a lengthy discussion of God's moral government and the central role played by the Scriptures in providing "a system of moral Laws, revealed to illustrate the glory of God, in the salvation of man." In what must have seemed like music to the ears of the Park Street congregation, Beecher then issued a stirring defense of the doctrine of the Trinity; the authority of the Bible; the need for repentance, faith,

---

of a third to a half of their total student bodies, which in those days usually numbered between a hundred and two hundred fifty" students. See pp. 39–44 for Orr's more detailed descriptions.

8. Cross, *Autobiography of Lyman Beecher*, 1:27–31.
9. Spring and Beecher quoted in Fitzmier, *New England's Moral Legislator*, 76–77.

and obedience; the reality of heaven and hell; and the centrality of justification by faith alone.

Finally—many pages into his manuscript—Beecher turned to Park Street's "Pastor Elect," Sereno Dwight, with some specific words of instruction. "My dear brother," he began, "you are about to take the pastoral care of this church and congregation. Their salvation," he continued, will either "be promoted or hindered by the instructions which you give, and the pastoral duties, which you perform or neglect." But do not be dismayed, he counseled, for "the reward of fidelity is as glorious as the punishment of treachery is dreadful; and with the Bible in your hand, and Jesus Christ with you always, you are thoroughly furnished, and can do all things."

"Your duty is plain," Beecher told the young ordinand: Read the Bible "daily as part of your devotion, and study it as a part of your profession"; remember that "yours is the office of an expositor of that divine book, and not of a legislator to revise and modify its sacred pages"; do not "be wise in your own conceit; and dare not to be wise above what is written"; treasure the creeds and confessions of historic orthodoxy but do not embrace any opinion until you are convinced that it is in full "agreement with the Scriptures"; declare "to your people the moral law," the reality of "their entire depravity" and the "danger" of "eternal punishment"; explain to your people "the nature of repentance, as the sorrow of holy love for sin; and the nature of faith, as the confidence of holy love in the Saviour." In short, he counseled, you must "dare to think for yourself," making sure in the process that you "give to others the same liberty." Finally, Beecher concluded, "Whatever may be your attainments in human science, your might in the Scriptures, your popularity as a preacher, or your estimation in the affections of your people," consider all of it as nothing "in comparison with their actual conversion to God. Set your heart upon the great blessing of a revival of religion. Desire it speedily and constantly. Pray for it without ceasing, and stir up the members of your Church to concentrate, on this point, the whole importunity of the prayer of faith. And live, and preach,

and pray, and act, in such a manner, as shall lay the best foundation to expect the blessing."[10]

Seldom have a preacher's words become more deeply embed-
ded in a young pastor's ministry than did Beecher's instructions to
Sereno Dwight at that early September gathering in 1817. "Set your
heart upon the great blessing of a revival of religion," Beecher had
counseled, echoing words that Sereno had likely heard on many
occasions from his own father, "and live, and preach, and pray, and
act, in such a manner" as to lay the foundation for God's blessing.[11]
Dwight was determined to do exactly that, even at risk to his own
health. By late in 1822 the blessings had arrived. If "[you] would
have the drops of heavenly grace descend upon any one," wrote
Rufus Anderson, the clerk of Park Street Church, "[you must] take
pains to bring that one under the heavenly cloud." During the early
months of the revival, Anderson reported, scores of new believers,
over half of whom were under the age of twenty, had experienced
for themselves "the drops of heavenly grace" and had been welcomed into Park Street Church as new members.[12] By the end of
1824, largely as a result of the revivals, a total of 120 new members
had been added to the rolls of Park Street Church, another 101 new
members had joined Old South Congregational Church and an
additional 62 new members had become part of Union Church on
Essex Street, a new orthodox congregation established in 1819.[13]

---

10. Lyman Beecher, *The Bible a Code of Laws, a sermon delivered in Park Street
    Church, Boston, September 3, 1817* . . . (Andover, MA: Flagg & Gould, 1818).
11. Beecher, *The Bible a Code of Laws*, see especially pages 43–46. For a helpful
    discussion of Beecher's theology see Douglas A. Sweeney, *Nathaniel Taylor,
    New Haven Theology, and the Legacy of Jonathan Edwards* (New York:
    Oxford University Press, 2003); Frank Hugh Foster, *A Genetic History of the
    New England Theology* (New York: Russell & Russell, 1963); and Sidney Earl
    Mead, *Nathaniel William Taylor 1786–1858: A Connecticut Liberal* (North
    Haven, CT: Archon Books, 1967).
12. Rufus Anderson, "Second Report of the Committee of Park Street Church,"
    a thirty-page handwritten report presented to the congregation at the eve-
    ning service on July 28, 1823. The original copy of this report can be found
    in the Ockenga Papers.
13. For prints of Park Street Church and Old South Congregational Church, see
    William H. Whitmore, "Abel Bowen," in *The Bostonian Society Publications,*
    vol. 1, *Boston Old State House 1886–1888* (Boston: T. R. Marvin & Sons,
    1888), 52.

The revival of 1822–24, followed by similar "seasons of refreshing" in 1826 and 1827 (during Edward Beecher's tenure as pastor—Park Street's third pastor and the son of Lyman Beecher), in 1831 and 1832 (during the ministry of Joel H. Linsley—Park Street's fourth pastor), and again in 1841 and 1842 (during the ministry of Silas Aiken—Park Street's fifth pastor), brought new energy and renewed hope to Boston's beleaguered evangelical community.[14] By the mid-1840s, as a result of these revivals, fourteen new Congregational churches, all ardently Trinitarian, had been planted in Boston—joining hands with Old South and Park Street in the cause of biblical orthodoxy and swelling its combined membership rolls to more than five thousand.[15] Hundreds of additional converts had also joined Baptist, Episcopal, Lutheran, Methodist, German Reformed, African Methodist Episcopal, and other denominations throughout the city—expanding Boston's evangelical presence to forty-five churches with over fourteen thousand members. In light of the enormous success that had been enjoyed by the Unitarians just a few years earlier, the resurgence of Trinitarian orthodoxy was nothing short of stunning.[16]

---

14. Edward Beecher served as pastor of Park Street Church from 1826 until 1830; Joel H. Linsley served as pastor from 1832 to 1835; and Silas Aiken served as pastor from 1837 to 1848. See H. Crosby Englizian, *Brimstone Corner: Park Street Church, Boston* (Chicago: Moody Press, 1968), 97–112, for pictures and descriptions of the revivals and of Park Street's first twelve pastors. The images can be found between pages 80 and 81. According to Moore, a total of 144 new members joined Park Street as a result of the 1822–1824 revivals; 134 were added as a result of the 1826–1827 revivals; and 337 as a result of the 1841–1842 revivals. See Martin Moore, *Boston Revival, 1842* (Wheaton, IL: R. O. Roberts, 1980), 34.

15. By 1842, according to Moore's figures, membership in these Congregational churches was as follows: Old South (502), Park Street (671), Essex Street (572), Bowdoin Street (671), Green Street (256), South Boston (251), Pine Street (278), Salem Street (587), Central Church (489), East Boston (80), Mariners' Church (173), Marlboro Chapel (210), Garden Street (182), and New Church (82). See Moore, *Boston Revival*, 67. Engravings and descriptions of some of these churches can be found in Whitmore, "Abel Bowen," 29–52.

16. "The increase of Orthodox churches in this city," observed Martin Moore in 1842, "has been in a great degree owing to the colonizing system. To advance the cause of evangelical religion, brethren of different churches have volunteered to go out and form new churches. God has greatly blessed these efforts." *Boston Revival*, 66.

"The commencement of the present century," Nathaniel Willis wrote, "found the Congregational churches of this city in a state of deep spiritual declension. The piety, fidelity and spirituality of the mass of her members were flickering like the light of a dying lamp. The Christianity of the day retained in its external forms and aspects much that was venerable and conservative, but its life and power were gone; the real, throbbing, earnest soul of it was stifled and palsied. The voice of the pulpit in force was not without strength and cogency, the decencies, charities and virtues of a high-toned morality, but seldom echoed the thunders of a violated law, or the melting accepts of Calvary. There were no revivals quickening the people of God," Willis observed, "awakening and converting the penitent, there were no associations in the midst of us to print and scatter tracts, to print Bibles, to undertake the conquest of the heathen world for Christ."[17] Then came the founding of Park Street Church in 1809—followed by the gracious outpouring of God's Spirit during the 1820s, 1830s, and 1840s—bringing new hope to Boston's evangelical community and literally changing the city's religious landscape. "The Lord hath done great things for us," Moore observed, borrowing the language of the Scriptures, "whereof we are glad." Therefore, he concluded, the church must commit "anew to the work, and never give over until the whole city is renovated."[18]

Preaching, Repentance, and Prayer

In these early nineteenth-century revivals, as throughout every era of Christian history, the three primary means that God has been pleased to bless in the sending of genuine revival remained the same: namely, the faithful proclamation of Holy Scripture, true repentance, and believing prayer.[19] These are the primary means,

---

17. Willis quoted in Ockenga, "The Unique and Unparalleled Position of Park Street Church," 12–13.
18. Moore, *Boston Revival*, 144. For descriptions of the various denominations involved and the number of new members that were added as a result of the revivals see pp. 68–134. See also Rudy Mitchell, *History of Revivalism in Boston* (Boston: Emmanuel Gospel Center, 2007), 19–29.
19. This pattern of biblical renewal comes from Scripture itself. See Walter C.

for example, that Rufus Anderson seems to highlight in his report on interviews conducted by Park Street's membership committee with ninety-three candidates who presented themselves for church membership in 1823—all ninety-three of whom had been converted as a result of the 1822–23 revivals. "We should take great pains to bring persons within hearing of plain, orthodox preaching," Anderson stressed, since "the *orthodox* doctrines appear to have been the only class of truths, which excited the candidates to attend to their eternal well-being." We need to be reminded "how little probability there is, that any one, who does not hear orthodox preaching, will ever be converted. Let it be forever engraved on our memories," he urged, "that whatever instruments man may use, the only instrument used by the Spirit, in convincing and converting men, is the *Word of God*, or, in other words, the *truths of the Gospel*." It is "the *public preaching* of the Gospel," the membership committee was convinced, that has been "of great importance" in sustaining these revivals. "Some have affected to undervalue public preaching, as a means of awakening sinners, especially during a revival of religion; and have maintained, that conferences, prayer meetings, and private conversations, were the most promising means of promoting a revival. No doubt these are highly important, and indeed indispensable," Anderson continued, "but among the number of those [interviewed by the committee] who can assign any particular cause of their awakening, a larger number assign public preaching as the cause, than either private meetings, or conversation. This is important," Anderson concluded, since "the *preached* Gospel is now, as it always has been, the grand ordinance in the economy of grace."[20]

While their individual experiences varied widely both with respect to "duration and degree," all ninety-three were aware of

---

Kaiser Jr., *Revive Us Again: Biblical Insights for Encouraging Spiritual Renewal* (Nashville: Broadman & Holman Publishers, 1999).

20. Rufus Anderson, "Second Report," 11–12. When the candidates for admission to membership were asked, as most of them were, "why they thought they should seek to live like Christians, in case there were no heaven and no hereafter, they all answered, that they should wish to live so, because of the superior happiness such a life afforded" (p. 26).

their own sinfulness and spiritual need. Although its expression took many forms, from a deep-seated fear of God's judgment to a profound attraction to the beauty of "Jesus Christ as an atoning sacrifice," the starting place for everyone was genuine repentance— the overwhelming sense of one's sinfulness and the determination (as the appropriate response of a grateful heart to God's amazing grace) to turn from sin and darkness and to embrace "an all-sufficient Savior."[21]

A "daily prayer meeting commenced in 1840," observed Park Street's twelfth pastor, that was "held at 8:30 in the morning six days a week" and "at which there were never less than thirty and sometimes as many as three hundred people united in prayer and testimony for an outpouring of the Holy Spirit upon the city of Boston." These meetings, Ockenga continued, "lasted for four years, during which time hundreds of people were taken into the cooperative Congregational churches on profession of faith and by letter. In one year alone seven hundred fifteen people were received on profession of faith. Park Street Church," he noted, "received over three hundred members as a result of these prayer meetings. They were the means of strengthening the newly formed churches which were being founded constantly by the Orthodox congregations."[22]

The Marks of Genuine Revival: The Edwards Legacy

While the revivals were welcomed by virtually everyone within Boston's growing evangelical community, they attracted an abundance of critics as well.[23] While some excesses undoubtedly

---

21. Ibid., 13.
22. Ockenga, "The Unique and Unparalleled Position of Park Street Church," 17–18.
23. A *revival*, as I have been using the term, is a renewal of spiritual vitality among God's people, always producing in the life of the believer a turning from sin, an obedience to Scripture, a deeper love for God, and a more active concern for one's neighbor. While God has been pleased to bless the prayers of his people, a genuine revival is always—from start to finish—the work of the sovereign God. An *awakening*, is a period of general revival within which the renewal of spiritual vitality is witnessed across traditional boundaries. Throughout its history, America has experienced hundreds of

occurred, as they had during the Great Awakening, the revivals at Park Street Church in large measure exhibited the same "distinguishing marks" of genuine revival that Jonathan Edwards had identified in his 1741 commencement address at Yale College. Using 1 John 4:1 as his text, Edwards had argued that even during the apostolic age, an era of Christian history that was marked by "the greatest outpouring of the Spirit of God that ever was," the "counterfeits did also then abound." Because "the Devil" has always been "abundant in mimicking both the ordinary and extraordinary influences of the Spirit of God" it was "necessary that the church of Christ should be furnished with some certain rules, and distinguishing and clear marks by which she might proceed safely in judging of spirits, and distinguish the true from the false, without danger of being imposed upon."[24]

Edwards then listed nine "negative signs," that is, "evidences" that might actually occur during the revivals but that do not of themselves either validate or invalidate the revivals as a genuine work of God: namely, (1) that the revival is carried on in a way that is "unusual or extraordinary"; (2) that the revival produces unusual "effects" on the body (i.e., "tears, trembling, groans, loud outcries, agonies of body or the failing of bodily strength"); (3) that the revival "produces a great deal of noise about religion"; (4) that the revival creates "many impressions" on the participants' "imaginations"; (5) that "means are made use of in producing" the revival (i.e., godly example, the use of reason, the preaching of God's Word, observation of others who have been awakened, including one's spouse, etc.); (6) that "many that seem to be the subjects" of the

---

revivals and perhaps four major periods of religious awakening. See Earle E. Cairns, *An Endless Line of Splendor: Revivals and Their Leaders from the Great Awakening to the Present* (Wheaton, IL: Tyndale House, 1986).

24. Jonathan Edwards, "The Distinguishing Marks of a Work of the Spirit of God," in *The Great Awakening*, ed. C. C. Goen, vol. 4, The Works of Jonathan Edwards (New Haven: Yale University Press, 1972), 226. The full text is found on pages 226–88. For an excellent introduction to the Great Awakening see Joseph Tracy, *The Great Awakening* (Edinburgh, U.K.: Banner of Truth, 1997); and for a collection of primary documents see Alan Heimert and Perry Miller, eds., *The Great Awakening* (Indianapolis: Bobbs-Merrill, 1967).

revival "are guilty of great imprudences and irregularities in their conduct"; (7) that "some delusions of Satan" are "intermixed with the work"; (8) that some who "were thought to be wrought upon, fall away into gross errors or scandalous practices"; and (9) that the revival "seems to be promoted by ministers insisting very much on the terrors of God's holy law, and that with a great deal of pathos and earnestness."

After listing these negative signs, Edwards turned his attention to the five "sure, distinguishing, Scripture evidences and marks of a work of the Spirit of God, by which we may proceed in judging of any operation we find in ourselves, or see among people, without danger of being misled"—namely, we know that a revival is genuine (1) when it "operates after such a manner, as to raise their esteem of that Jesus that was born of the Virgin, and was crucified without the gates of Jerusalem; and seems more to confirm and establish their minds in the truth of what the Gospel declares to us of his being the Son of God, and the Saviour of men"; (2) when it lessens "the lust of the flesh, and the lust of the eyes, and the pride of life" and promotes an "earnest seeking" for "the kingdom of God and his righteousness"; (3) when it produces "a greater regard to the Holy Scriptures"; (4) when it leads "persons to truth, convincing them of those things that are true"; and (5) when it produces "a spirit of love to God and man."[25]

These distinguishing marks, as reflected in the writings of Edwards, not only characterized the remarkable revivals that touched Park Street throughout its early years but they also became, in a sense, the core beliefs that have sustained congregational life throughout Park Street's long and distinguished history— namely, its belief in the triune God: Father, Son, and Holy Spirit; its conviction that the only remedy for sin is Christ's atoning work on the cross; its certainty that we are all sinners in need of conversion; its commitment to the unique and final authority of the Bible and our need to obey its teachings in every area of life and work; and its conviction that Christ has commissioned us to

---

25. Edwards, "Distinguishing Marks," 226–88.

spread the "good news," to build His church, to live lives of truth and integrity, to stand for justice, to care for the needy, to love our neighbors, and to continue Christ's work here on earth until we are welcomed into heaven to live forever with the sovereign Lord.

The Later Revivals

Given the importance of these religious revivals in the early history of Park Street, it should come as no surprise to discover that religious revivals have remained a prominent part of the congregation's life throughout its later history as well. While scores of smaller "harvests," as Solomon Stoddard liked to call them, could be cited, six major periods of religious awakening are worthy of special mention: The famous "Prayer Revival" of 1856, 1857, and 1858 (involving Charles G. Finney);[26] the "Boston Revival of 1877" (involving Dwight L. Moody);[27] "Boston's Awakening" of 1909 (involving J. Wilbur Chapman and Charles M. Alexander);[28] the "Billy Sunday Revival" of 1916 and 1917;[29] the "New England Mid-Century Revival" of 1950 (involving

---

26. See Kathryn Teresa Long, *The Revival of 1857–58: Interpreting an American Religious Awakening* (New York: Oxford University Press, 1998); Wilbur M. Smith, "The Fulton Street Prayer Meeting and the Great Revival," in the *Sunday School Times* (June 1, 1957); Charles E. Hambrick-Stowe, *Charles G. Finney and the Spirit of American Evangelicalism* (Grand Rapids: Eerdmans, 1996); and Garth M. Rosell, "Charles G. Finney: His Place in the Stream of American Evangelicalism," in Leonard I. Sweet, ed., *The Evangelical Tradition in America* (Macon, GA: Mercer University Press, 1997), 131–47.

27. H. M. Grout, ed., *The Gospel Invitation: Sermons Related to the Boston Revival of 1877* (Boston: Lockwood, Brooks, and Company, 1877); Lyle W. Dorsett, *A Passion for Souls: The Life of D. L. Moody* (Chicago: Moody Press, 1997); William R. Moody, *The Life of Dwight L. Moody* (New York: Revell, 1900); and Garth M. Rosell, ed., *Commending the Faith: The Preaching of Dwight L. Moody* (Peabody, MA: Hendrickson, 1999).

28. Arcturus Z. Conrad, *Boston's Awakening: A Complete Account of the Great Boston Revival* (Boston: King's Business, 1909); and Margaret Lamberts Bendroth, *Fundamentalists in the City: Conflict and Division in Boston's Churches, 1885–1950* (New York: Oxford University Press, 2005), 127–40.

29. Lyle W. Dorsett, *Billy Sunday and the Redemption of Urban America* (Grand Rapids: Eerdmans, 1991); and Bendroth, *Fundamentalists in the City*, 141–54.

Billy Graham);[30] and Boston's "Quiet Revival" during the early years of the new millennium.[31]

While the well-known nineteenth-century evangelist Charles G. Finney had preached in Boston during 1832 and again during 1843, his 1856 meetings proved to be his most successful. Andrew Leete Stone, the sixth pastor of Park Street, had invited Finney to come for a series of meetings at the church.[32] For nearly five months, between December 7, 1856 and April 19, 1857, Finney filled Park Street's pulpit twice each Sunday, every Friday morning and four evenings each week while his wife, Elizabeth, held special meetings for women.[33]

"The first sermon that I preached," Finney reported, "was directed to the searching of the church; for I always began by trying to stir up a thorough and all-pervading interest among professors of religion; to secure the reclaiming of those that were backslidden, and search out those that were self-deceived, and if possible bring them to Christ." After the service, as Finney and Stone were conversing near the pulpit, the pastor turned to the evangelist and said, "Brother Finney, I wish to have you understand that I need to have this preaching as much as any member of this church. I have been

30. *Revival in Our Time: The Story of the Billy Graham Evangelistic Campaigns, Including Six of His Sermons* (Wheaton, IL: Van Kampen Press, 1950); Garth M. Rosell, "America's Hour Has Struck," *Christian History and Biography,* Fall 2006, 12–19; J. Edwin Orr, *The Second Evangelical Awakening in America* (London: Marshall, Morgan & Scott, 1952), 160–211; Joel A. Carpenter, *Revive Us Again: The Reawakening of American Fundamentalism* (New York: Oxford University Press, 1997), 211–32; and Bendroth, *Fundamentalists in the City,* 177–90.

31. Rudy Mitchell, "An Introduction to Boston's Quiet Revival," in *Emmanuel Research Review* (June 7, 2004).

32. Andrew Leete Stone (1815–1892), a graduate of Yale in 1837, served as Park Street's pastor from 1849 until 1866 when he moved to San Francisco. See Edwin M. Bacon, *King's Dictionary of Boston* (Cambridge, MA: King, 1883), 351.

33. For Finney's own account of these meetings, see Garth M. Rosell and Richard A. G. Dupuis, eds., *The Memoirs of Charles G. Finney: The Complete Restored Text* (Grand Rapids: Zondervan, 1989), 559–72. The quotations in the following paragraphs are also from this book, 559–60. While Finney also preached in several other Boston area churches, his primary work was carried out at Park Street.

very much dissatisfied with my religious state for a long time; and have sent for you on my own account, and for the sake of my own soul, as well as for the sake of the souls of the people."

Stone's disarming honesty left a deep impression on Finney—and it became increasingly clear that Finney's preaching was having a profound impact upon Stone. As the meetings progressed, Finney later reported, "This brother became more and more deeply convicted, until one day he sent a note to my lodgings inviting me to his study that he might have some conversation with me. He then told me that he thought he had been self-deceived. That when he was in College he passed through a change that he was led to think was conversion; but he was now satisfied that he was entirely mistaken and that he had never been truly converted; and that he wished me to give him the same directions that I would to any other person in his situation." The two began "a protracted and very interesting conversation," Finney continued, and "I found his convictions of sin very striking. He seemed then to thoroughly give his heart to God." That evening, at a prayer meeting in the vestry, and the following Sunday as a part of his sermon, Stone related his experience to his Park Street parishioners, explaining to them that he had at last been truly converted.

These revelations, Finney reported, "produced a very deep impression upon the church and congregation, and upon the city quite extensively. Some of the pastors thought that it was injudicious for him to make a thing of that kind so public. But I did not regard it in that light." Indeed, Finney concluded, it became the very "best means he could use for the salvation of his people" and it was "highly calculated to produce among professors of religion generally a very great searching of heart."[34] For his part, Stone remained deeply grateful to his spiritual mentor. "My personal indebtedness to you is beyond all compass of expression," he later wrote in a letter to Finney, "for good to my own soul—for more certain and

---

34. Rosell and Dupuis, *The Memoirs of Charles G. Finney*, 559–60. Reports of Finney's Boston meetings were carried in the *Congregationalist* (Boston), the *Oberlin Evangelist*, the *New York Observer*, the *New-York Evangelist*, the *Independent* (New York), and the *British Standard* (London).

copious views of the sufficiency of Christ for every soul's need—
and for wise suggestions as to the way to preach Christ to my dying
fellow men."[35]

Although Finney's ministry at Park Street was concluded by
mid-April of 1857, throngs of eager listeners continued to pack the
sanctuary to hear the preaching of Andrew Stone. The delighted
parish was "compelled to order a cord or two of camp stools," as
Abraham Hale has recounted the story, to accommodate the crowds.
Appealing to "the reason, as well as to the conscience," Stone seemed
to be able to bring fresh life to even "the oldest and most thread-
bare topic." His preaching was "always brief, never wearisome" and
he had "a fine presence, a wonderful voice, and a great ease in his
delivery." While "Orthodox" to the core, Hale concluded, Dr. Stone
seemed always to exhibit a "catholicity of spirit."[36]

In the summer of 1862, as divisions between the North and the
South continued to deepen, President Abraham Lincoln issued a call
for troops.[37] In response to his call, the Forty-fifth Massachusetts
Regiment was formed and Andrew Stone consented to serve as its
chaplain. In addition, eighty young men from Park Street volunteered to enlist. Eight of them, as the moving memorials behind
Park Street's pulpit attest, did not return. "There are few scenes on
earth that reveal more visibly the glory of the Divine presence and
the power of sustaining grace than the deathbed of a Christian,"
Stone observed in a letter to the Park Street congregation. "One
of our own Boston boys, a member of Company A," told him that
during "the battle of Kinston, under that terrible fire of the enemy,
his Saviour came to him as never before, declared His Presence,
revealed His love, and held his soul in His hands." Although his

---

35. A. L. Stone to C. G. Finney, November 27, 1858, Charles G. Finney Papers,
    microfilm, roll 4, Oberlin College Archives, Oberlin, Ohio.
36. Abraham G. R. Hale, "Chaplain Stone and the Religious Life of the Forty-
    fifth Massachusetts Regiment," in *History of the Forty-fifth Regiment*, ed.
    Albert W. Mann (Boston: Wallace Spooner, 1908), 223–34, copy in the Park
    Street Church archives. Hale was a private in Company A.
37. For some fascinating background reading, see Mark A. Noll, *The Civil War
    as a Theological Crisis* (Chapel Hill: University of North Carolina Press,
    2006).

lungs were congested so that he could only speak "by gasps and whispers," Stone continued, "he held my face down close to his" and "told me that he never had had full assurance of his pardon and acceptance" with God until "he became a soldier." Then, with the Lord's Prayer on his lips, he slipped gently into eternity. "How could a Christian life close more appropriately and triumphantly?" he reflected. "If any man ever doubted the sufficiency of the gospel of Christ to transform, sustain and elevate a human life, and help it to meet its last and greatest need, let him look upon such a scene, and his skepticism must vanish like mist before the sun." Stone appealed to Park Street congregation at the close of the letter, "Let your prayers hover constantly over the pillows of our sick and wounded. The touch of loved fingers is far away, but your intercessions may be as the shadow of an angel's wing to faces growing white under the signature of death."[38]

Major revivals, as Gardiner Shattuck has noted, broke out during the Civil War both within the Union and the Confederate ranks.[39] Under the leadership of chaplains such as Andrew Stone, "between 100,000 and 200,000" Union soldiers and "approximately 150,000" Confederate troops were converted to Christ. Preaching and praying often continued around the clock, according to some reports, and scores of chapels had to be built to accommodate all the soldiers who wanted to attend.[40]

The revivals of America's Civil War were followed by a fresh surge of spiritual renewal within many of Boston's churches. "The revival

---

38. Letter from Andrew Stone to the Park Street Church congregation (February 12, 1863), writing from New Berne, North Carolina. A copy of Stone's letter is included in Hale, "Park Street in the Civil War," in *History of the Forty-fifth Regiment,* ed. Albert W. Mann (Boston: Wallace Spooner, 1908), 25–26. See also Andrew L. Stone, "War: The Romance and the Reality: A Memorial Address by Chaplain A. L. Stone," in *History of the Forty-fifth Regiment,* 314–25.

39. See Gardiner H. Shattuck Jr., "Revivals in the Camp," *Christian History,* issue 33, *The Untold Story of Christianity and the Civil War* 11, no. 1 (1992): 28–31. See also idem, *A Shield and Hiding Place: The Religious Life of the Civil War Armies* (Macon, GA: Mercer University Press, 1987).

40. "Christianity and the Civil War: Did You Know?" *Christian History,* issue 33, *The Untold Story of Christianity and the Civil War* 11, no. 1 (1992): 1.

now in progress," as the Congregational minister Henry Grout reported in April of 1877, is "still a rising tide."[41] The public meetings not only engaged the energies of scores of pastors throughout the region but also involved many of the leaders of the Young Men's Christian Association and even some faculty members from New England's educational institutions. The primary focus of the revivals, however, tended to be upon the preaching of Dwight L. Moody and the music of Ira Sankey.[42] "In Boston, as in Chicago," William Moody observed, "a large temporary building was erected for the mission, with a seating capacity of six thousand. A representative committee of prominent ministers and laymen of all denominations supported the work, and from the first great interest was shown." For over two months, "often twice or thrice a day," the evangelist's son reported, the "building was filled to copious overflowing."[43] Moody's ministry in Boston, coupled with similar efforts in Brooklyn, Philadelphia, New York, and Chicago from 1875 to 1877, marked the beginning of his twenty-year evangelistic mission in America. "By almost every angle of vision," historian Lyle Dorsett has argued, "Boston was another great success. Hundreds of thousands attended the meetings," he continued, "thousands made commitments of faith in Christ, and many churches gained new members."[44]

Among the churches that benefited the most, of course, was Park Street Church. That it did so should hardly be surprising. After all, as Englizian has reminded us, the Moody campaign not only "had its origin in a meeting held in the Park Street Church vestry on

41. Grout, *Gospel Invitation*, 3–4.
42. For a listing of pastors and educational institutions (including Wellesley College, Harvard College, Boston University, Andover Theological Seminary, the Newton Theological Institution, and the Episcopal Theological School), see Grout, *Gospel Invitation*, 3–6.
43. W. R. Moody, *The Life of Dwight L. Moody*, 292. Moody had been converted in Boston, some two decades earlier, while working in his uncle's shoe store. For a brief description of his conversion and subsequent ministry see my introduction to *Commending the Faith*. Dr. Paul Toms, Park Street's thirteenth pastor, has called the simple brass plaque that marks the spot of Moody's conversion the single most important historical landmark in Boston. For the location of the building, see Mitchell, *History of Revivalism in Boston*, 34.
44. Dorsett, *A Passion for Souls*, 254.

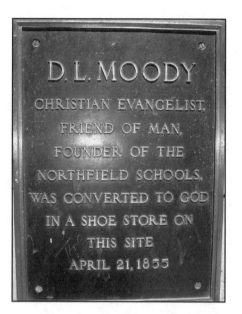

Plaque commemorating the
conversion of D. L. Moody,
Boston, April 21, 1855.
Photograph by the author.

April 15, 1876," but many of its leaders and members worked tire-
lessly to ensure its success. Park Street, in fact, served as host to
some of the "numerous daily prayer meetings conducted throughout the city" and on occasion it even suspended some of its regular
services so that its members could attend the Moody meetings.[45]
The meetings emphasized the "union of churches, preaching and
singing services, inquiry rooms, Bible-reading sessions, and special
meetings for men, women, children, and people who sensed a calling to full-time ministry."[46] In addition, as Mitchell has observed, it
engaged hundreds of Christians throughout the region in a special
ministry to the city's poor, dispossessed, and needy. These efforts
to extend the ministry to urban families, often by door-to-door
visitation, "was a strategy Moody felt was necessary to reach those
in the large cities who would not come out to church."[47]

---

45. Englizian, *Brimstone Corner*, 186. It was on that occasion that fifteen men
   gathered at Park Street "to consider a proposed invitation to the evangelist.
   On the following May 8, a conference of representatives from seventy-eight
   evangelical churches voted to invite Moody to Boston."
46. Dorsett, *A Passion for Souls*, 250.
47. Mitchell, *History of Revivalism in Boston*, 35.

Difficult Times at Park Street Church

Despite the obvious encouragement that the Moody/Sankey meetings brought to many of Park Street's members, however, the last quarter of the nineteenth century proved to be a difficult and discouraging time for the church.[48] The terrible loss of life during the Civil War, coupled with the enormous loss of homes and jobs that followed in the wake of the great fire that swept through a large section of the city in 1872, left many of Boston's citizens in difficult circumstances and with painful memories.

Added to these concerns was the "Fight for Boston Common," as historian Margaret Bendroth has described the growing tensions between Protestants and Roman Catholics throughout the city.[49] A staunchly Protestant community during its early years, Boston by the late nineteenth century had become remarkably diverse—due, in large measure, to the burgeoning immigrant populations that chose to make the city their new home.[50] Marcus Lee Hansen has suggested that beginning in the 1880s, immigration tended to bring an increasing number of Roman Catholics to America's shores.[51] By 1900, the growing presence of Irish, Italian, and French-Canadian immigrants—many of whom were at least nominally Roman Catholic—had made Boston into the nation's second largest Roman Catholic archdiocese. In addition, as Boston's Protestant community was clearly aware, the Irish Catholics had

---

48. See Englizian, "Years of Decline" and "The Low-Water Mark," in *Brimstone Corner*, 190–209.
49. For a fascinating analysis see Bendroth, *Fundamentalists in the City*, 41–83, 170–76.
50. Sam Bass Warner Jr., *Streetcar Suburbs: The Process of Growth in Boston, 1870–1900* (Cambridge, MA: Harvard University Press, 1962); Thomas H. O'Connor, *Bibles, Brahmins and Bosses: A Short History of Boston* (Boston: Trustees of the Public Library of the City of Boston, 1991); Stephan Thernstrom, *The Other Bostonians: Poverty and Progress in the American Metropolis, 1880–1970* (Cambridge, MA: Harvard University Press, 1973); Oscar Handlin, *The Uprooted* (New York: Grosset & Dunlap, 1951); and Aaron Abell, *The Urban Impact on American Protestantism, 1865–1900* (Cambridge, MA: Harvard University Press, 1943).
51. See Marcus Lee Hansen, *The Immigrant in American History* (New York: Harper Torchbook, 1964), 3–29. Compare John Higham, *Strangers in the Land: Patterns of American Nativism, 1860–1925* (New York: Atheneum, 1966).

begun to play an increasingly important role in the city's political life.[52]

Further complicating matters was a series of problems that had emerged within the church under the pastoral leadership of William H. H. Murray (1868–1874), John L. Withrow (1876–1887 and 1898–1907), David Gregg (1887–1890), and Isaac J. Lansing (1893–1897). Murray's pastorate, for example, had deeply divided the congregation. His outspoken views and relatively freewheeling style brought him into almost immediate conflict with many of Park Street's leading members. By 1874, the gifted but controversial preacher was gone.[53] "For the first time in nearly three quarters of a century, there was grave unpleasantness in the church."[54]

As if the troubles with Murray had not been sufficient, a fresh controversy broke out within the congregation shortly after John L. Withrow was installed as Murray's successor.[55] Within months of his arrival, Withrow had appointed a committee to revise the congregation's historic Articles of Faith and Constitution. Although Withrow certainly had no intention of undermining Park Street's doctrinal foundations, his attempt to update a document that had stood unchanged for sixty-eight years was interpreted by some as exactly that.[56]

Adding to these concerns, moreover, was the fact that increasing numbers of Park Street members were abandoning the city for what they hoped would be a better life in the burgeoning suburbs. This

---

52. See Sam Bass Warner Jr., "A Brief History of Boston," in *Mapping Boston,* ed. Alex Krieger and David Cobb (Cambridge, MA: MIT Press, 2001), 8.

53. For a discussion of Murray's ministry at Park Street Church, extending from 1868 to 1874, see Englizian, "The Great Innovator," in *Brimstone Corner,* 164–77; and Bendroth, *Fundamentalists in the City,* 159–61.

54. Arcturus Z. Conrad, *Commemorative Exercises at the One Hundredth Anniversary of the Organization of Park Street Church* (Boston: Park Street Centennial Committee, 1909).

55. Dr. John L. Withrow, formerly pastor of the Second Presbyterian Church in Indianapolis, Indiana, actually served as Park Street's pastor on two separate occasions, from 1876–1887 and again from 1898–1907. For a discussion of his ministry at Park Street see Englizian, *Brimstone Corner,* 178–89.

56. See "Dr. Withrow's Farewell," in *The Congregationalist,* January 6, 1887, 5, as a reflection of the high regard in which he came to be held both within the church and in the larger community.

Title page from Park Street Church Articles of
Faith and Covenant, 1850. Courtesy of Park
Street Church.

pattern of urban flight, in turn, began to eat away at the congregation's membership rolls, its pew rents and its regular attendance.
Park Street's membership, for example, plummeted from 1,100 in
1886 to 366 in 1901—during the ministerial tenures of Withrow,
Gregg, and Lansing.[57] The growing financial crisis, moreover,
forced Park Street's leadership to remodel its basement, remov-
ing the burial crypts that had been housed there, so that it could
rent the space to a commercial florist and fruit grocer. By the turn
of the century the crisis had become so severe that many in the
congregation were convinced that the only solution was the sale or
lease of the property and the relocation of the congregation in the
suburbs.

The public response to this radical solution was immediate and
strong. "The interest in Park Street Church is not due to great antiq-
uity or wealth of historic associations like the Old South Church,
although 'America' was sung there for the first time and the church
has a unique place in Boston traditions," wrote Prescott F. Hall,
secretary of the newly constituted "Committee for the Preservation

---

57. The decline was during the period from 1886 to 1901. A helpful graph of
    shifts in Park Street's membership between 1885 and 1960 can be found in
    Bendroth, *Fundamentalists in the City*, 165.

of Park Street Church." Rather, he continued, "[our] chief interest lies in the fact that the church is an impressive architectural
monument, situated at a strategic point in the landscape of the city
and constituting a beautiful and time-honored feature of Boston,
indissolubly bound up with the very thought of Boston in every
mind."[58] Largely as a result of this community pressure, coupled
with the fund-raising efforts that it helped to inspire, the building
was saved. The congregation, however, to borrow John Bunyan's
classic phrase, ended its first century of ministry in "the slough of
despond."[59]

Reflecting on the first century of Park Street's history, one
is struck by a strange irony: namely, that Park Street's efforts to
enlarge the region's evangelical community—through its coura-
geous commitment to biblical orthodoxy and a church planting
strategy that Martin Moore has called their "colonizing system"—
created scores of new (and potentially competing) congregations
with which evangelical Christians could identify.[60] Consequently,
as increasing numbers of Park Street families moved to the suburbs
or to other parts of the city, they often became active in one of Park
Street's daughter congregations located closer to home. Park Street's
staunch commitment to this larger vision throughout its history, a
significant achievement to be sure, has not been without its corre-
sponding costs. During the late nineteenth century, in particular,

---

58. A copy of the response of the Committee for the Preservation of Park Street
Church, issued February 7, 1903, can be found in the Park Street Church
archives.

59. John Bunyan, *The Pilgrim's Progress* (1678; repr., New York: Oxford University Press, 2003), 16.

60. See Moore, *Boston's Revival*, 66. "To advance the cause of evangelical religion, brethren of different churches have volunteered to go out and form
new churches. God has greatly blessed these efforts." Harold John Ockenga
later commented: "Statistics tell us that in the year 1843 the thirteen new
orthodox churches [in Boston] had a larger average attendance than the
seventeen former churches that had defected to Unitarianism. Moreover,
in the seventy years following the founding of Park Street Church forty
new churches were established of which twenty-six were in ancient Boston
and fourteen in the suburbs. . . . In a real sense [Park Street] became the
mother of other churches of the orthodox belief." Ockenga, "The Unique
and Unparalleled Position of Park Street Church," 19–20.

these convictions left Park Street (like many other urban congregations) struggling for its very existence.

Cooperative Evangelism: Chapman, Sunday, and Graham

Despite these apparent drawbacks, Park Street Church has never abandoned its long-standing commitment to evangelical ecumenism. "This church has not been built, I trust, from party zeal, or ill will to our brethren," Edward Griffin declared at the dedication of Park Street Church in 1810. Indeed, he continued, "the worship of God, as conducted in this house, will not, I hope, wear the appearance of controversy; much less, of bitterness against others; but of meekness, rather, and gentleness, as the spirit of the gospel dictates. This pulpit was not erected to hurl anathemas against men who to their own master must stand or fall. But here, with an eye uplifted to heaven, and filled with tears, we are to make supplication for ourselves, our families, our brethren, and for a world lying in wickedness."[61]

This spirit of "meekness" and "gentleness" is clearly evident in Park Street's historic commitment to join hands with like-minded believers throughout New England and around the world in the spread of the gospel and the renewal of the church. Such cooperation, in fact, was a central feature of the Boston Awakening of 1909, the Billy Sunday meetings in 1916–17 and New England's Mid-Century Revival of 1950. Descriptions of these more recent revivals can be found in abundance.[62] The Boston Awakening of 1909 helped to bring new life and hope to many discouraged congregations throughout New England. The month-long series of meetings, chaired by Park Street's pastor, Arcturus

---

61. Edward D. Griffin, *A Sermon, Preached Jan. 10, 1810*, 18–19.
62. For the Chapman/Alexander meetings in 1909, see Conrad, *Boston's Awakening*; for the Billy Sunday meetings in 1916–17, see Bendroth, *Fundamentalists in the City*, 141–54; and for the Mid-Century Awakening, see Rosell, "America's Hour Has Struck"; Carpenter, *Revive Us Again*, 211–32; and Garth M. Rosell, *The Surprising Work of God: Harold John Ockenga, Billy Graham and the Rebirth of Evangelicalism* (Grand Rapids: Baker, 2008).

Zodiac Conrad, and known as the Greater Boston Simultaneous Campaign, was conducted in scores of churches throughout the region by twenty-seven different evangelists.[63] Although the central services, which began on January 26 and continued over the next four weeks, were held twice each day at Tremont Temple, virtually all of the evangelical churches in Boston and congregations in over twenty cities around the hub were strengthened as a result of the meetings. "In all my twenty-six years of ministry," Chapman later wrote, "I have never had such joy in preaching the Gospel as in the city of Boston for almost four weeks. All classes and conditions of people gave me the very best of hearing," he observed, "and I had the joy of seeing a great host turn unto Jesus Christ and accept Him as their Savior." It was "the greatest experience of my life."[64]

A similar spirit of cooperation also characterized the Billy Sunday meetings in 1916–17 and the New England Mid-Century Revival of 1950. Encouraged by friends like Allan C. Emery Jr. and Charles E. Fuller, for example, Harold John Ockenga, Park Street's twelfth pastor, had invited Billy Graham to Boston for a New Year's Eve youth rally at the six-thousand-seat Mechanics Hall in Boston to be followed by a nine-day evangelistic series to be held at Park Street Church. Emery, whose own father had been instrumental in bringing Billy Sunday to Boston a generation earlier, agreed to serve as general chairman for the meetings. The meetings, according to the *Boston Daily Globe*, were sponsored by "more than 100 local Protestant churches" in cooperation with the New England Fellowship, the Evangelistic Association of New England (now

---

63. The evangelists were J. Wilbur Chapman, J. W. Waddell, C. P. Schaeffer, A. W. Spooner, J. H. Elliott, T. Needham, Ralph Atkinson, F. Granstaff, Harry Taylor, E. E. Davidson, R. C. Norton, W. F. Stewart, H. W. Stough, H. N. Faulconer, G. R. Stair, W. Asher, O. S. Gray, A. J. Smith, M. S. Rees, Evangeline Booth, S. M. Sayford, J. A. Earl, F. C. Ottman, J. O. Buswell, H. D. Sheldon, D. S. Toy, and J. E. Thacker. Pictures of the evangelists can be found in the front section of Conrad, *Boston's Awakening.*
64. J. Wilbur Chapman, foreword to *Boston's Awakening: A Complete Account of the Great Boston Revival*, ed. Arcturus Z. Conrad (Boston: King's Business, 1909), 1.

Vision New England), and Youth for Christ.[65] As the appointed
time approached, however, even the most optimistic could not
have imagined the events that were about to take place. The young
preacher who had been scheduled to lead the crusade, the thirty-
one-year-old Billy Graham, was then largely unknown, at least
within the churches of New England.[66] His enormously successful
eight-week Crusade in Los Angeles had just ended, of course, but
expectations in Boston remained surprisingly modest and public-
ity was sparse.[67]

The New Year's Eve service at Mechanics Hall, however, changed
everything. The six thousand who jammed the hall, along with
the hundreds of people who were turned away, suddenly made the
event front-page news on January 1, 1950: "Evangelist Graham
Draws 6000," proclaimed the *Boston Herald*, and "more than could
be counted hit the sawdust trail," reported the *Boston Globe*. The
Boston Post, in its Sunday edition, carried a full report of the four-
hour meeting along with a detailed description of the service, a
listing of its major participants and a dramatic picture of the crowd
that had filled Mechanics Hall to overflowing.[68] One of the speakers that evening was Harold John Ockenga. In his comments, he
told the huge crowd that they were standing at a decisive moment
in history. What Boston was experiencing, Ockenga observed,

65. See the *Boston Daily Globe*, December 30, 1949, 5; and January 10, 1950, 1,
    34; and William C. Martin, *A Prophet with Honor* (New York: W. Morrow
    and Co., 1991), 123–41. By April of 1950, the publishers of Van Kampen
    Press had produced a fascinating little book, *Revival in Our Time: The Story
    of the Billy Graham Evangelistic Campaigns* (Wheaton, IL: Van Kampen
    Press, 1950), with help from Charles E. Fuller, Harold John Ockenga, C.
    Wade Freeman, J. Edwin Orr, Mel Larson, Don Hoke, Jerry Bevan, and Cliff
    Barrows. For the Boston revival, see especially pp. 28–33.
66. The *Boston Globe*, in its issues from March 26 to April 4, 1950, published
    a ten-part series on "The Life Story of Billy Graham" written by Joseph F.
    Dinneen. The *Boston Post*, on January 13, 14, and 15, 1950, published a
    three-part series on Dr. Graham's life written by Allen Thomason, and later
    produced an eight-page *Boston Post Souvenir Edition* on the "Life Story of
    Rev. Billy Graham," 165,000 copies of which it distributed free of charge.
67. The total attendance at Billy Graham's Los Angeles Crusade was an esti-
    mated 350,000 (with approximately 3,000 conversions). See Martin, *A
    Prophet with Honor*, 106–20.
68. The *Boston Post*, January 1, 1950, 15.

Harold John Ockenga welcoming the Billy Graham team, 1949. From left:
Grady Wilson, Harold John Ockenga, Billy Graham, Cliff Barrows, and Carlton
Booth. Photograph courtesy of Park Street Church.

was nothing short of the kind of "surprising work of God" that
had come to New England two centuries earlier under the ministry of George Whitefield and Jonathan Edwards. The linkage
with Edwards and Whitefield is significant. By "revival," Ockenga
argued, "I do not mean what we have often called revivals in the
churches, where we set up a meeting and bring in a preacher and
call it a 'revival.' I am talking now about a heaven-sent, Holy Ghost
revival given in the sovereignty of God with no human explanation
for it whatsoever."[69]

What came to be called the New England Mid-Century Revival
took place in two distinct phases: from December 31 to January 16
and from March 17 to April 23. The first phase was held exclusively
in Boston. When Graham returned in March and April, however,
the work fanned out to touch the major cities of all six New England
states. The climax came in a series of services that were held at the
Boston Garden followed by a final service held on Sunday afternoon

---

69. Harold John Ockenga, "Is America's Revival Breaking?" in *United Evangelical
Action* 9, no. 10 (July 1, 1950): 3–4, 8, 13–15. Transcribed address delivered at
the Eighth Annual Convention of the National Association of Evangelicals
in Indianapolis, April 18, 1950, Ockenga Papers.

at the Boston Common.[70] By the time both phases of the crusade had ended, nearly 300,000 had attended the meetings and over 9,000 had made public professions of faith in Christ.[71]

Boston's Quiet Revival

Given the prominent role that religious revivals have played throughout the history of Park Street Church, is there not reason to expect that similar seasons of refreshment will mark the congregation's future as well? Indeed, growing numbers of Christians throughout New England have been joining hands in a great "concert of prayer" that God will pour out His blessings upon this region once again. Others have been preparing themselves—through heartfelt repentance of their sins, by joining with other Christians in united, believing prayer, and through the faithful proclamation of and active obedience to the Word of God. While recognizing that all genuine revival is a gift from above, to use the language of Harold John Ockenga, it is always appropriate to pray with expectancy for the gentle refreshment of "a heaven-sent, Holy Ghost revival given in the sovereignty of God with no human explanation for it whatsoever."

What does not seem to be appropriate, however, is to expect that spiritual awakening will look exactly as it has in the past or come in precisely the same manner as has been true in earlier years. There is reason to believe that Park Street Church may, even now, be in the midst of a mighty spiritual awakening. In fact, all the marks of genuine revival—so powerfully expressed by Jonathan Edwards almost three hundred years ago—are also present in the life of the

70. While hundreds of photos were taken of this event, to my knowledge only one set of moving pictures was taken of the Boston Common gathering. My father, Merv Rosell, described by his good friend Billy Graham in a *Boston Globe* interview as "one of the greatest evangelists preaching today," had come to Boston to attend the final week of the meetings. Seeing the enormous crowd that had gathered, Cliff Barrows handed Dad his Bell and Howell camera and asked him to get some pictures of the service. This historic film is now housed with the Merv Rosell Papers at Gordon-Conwell Theological Seminary, South Hamilton, Massachusetts.
71. Harold Lindsell, *Park Street Prophet* (Wheaton, IL: Van Kampen Press, 1951), 155–56.

congregation today: Jesus is worshipped and adored as the Son of God and the Savior of the world; the Scriptures are treasured and faithfully proclaimed; there is clear evidence among many of a hungering and thirsting after righteousness; women, men, boys, and girls are being led to God's truth; and there is, in the very center of congregational life, a deep desire to love God with heart, soul, mind, and strength and to love the neighbor as we love ourselves. Indeed, every week of the year, literally thousands of Christ's followers (many of whom are brand-new believers) from scores of different nations, social classes, races, educational backgrounds, ages, interests, and vocations—pour into Park Street's historic walls for worship, fellowship, training, and accountability and then back out into the community to serve a needy world with energy, creativity, justice, compassion, and love. If these are not the marks of a spiritually renewed congregation, then it is difficult to know where one might look to find one.

It may well be, in fact, that Boston itself is experiencing what some have called a quiet revival. "Boston's church community has experienced a remarkable transformation during the last 35 years," observed Rudy Mitchell, a researcher at Boston's Emmanuel Gospel Center. While many mainline urban churches were closing their doors, hundreds of thriving new churches were being planted by wave upon wave of new immigrants from Haiti, Latin America, the Caribbean, and various parts of Asia and Africa. These new congregations, in conjunction with many of Boston's older African American churches, as Doug and Judy Hall have observed, appear to be in the midst of such a revival—labeled "quiet," as Mitchell explained, since "it was often not seen or heard by the larger church community and the public media. It was not seen in large stadium crusade meetings or in the building of dozens of mega-church buildings. Many of the new churches have met in urban storefront buildings or in shared space with other churches."[72]

---

72. Rudy Mitchell, "An Introduction to Boston's Quiet Revival"; and Douglas Hall, "How to Make Our 'Love in Action' Effective," both articles in the *Emmanuel Research Review*, June 7, 2004, published by the Emmanuel Gospel Center in Boston. See also Mitchell, *History of Revivalism in Boston*.

Similar revivals are breaking out in hundreds of communities around the globe.[73] "Growth similar to Boston's," observed Fuller Theological Seminary's Senior Professor of Church Growth Eddie Gibbs, "has been seen in other urban centers where changing demographics have brought populations with 'a more dynamic understanding of faith and church.' Such churches won't become visible," Gibbs observed, "without risking a loss of the energy they've found outside the mainstream. The question," Gibbs concluded, "is 'How do you remain cross-culturally engaged, without being culturally subverted?'"[74]

Such movements, of course, are not limited to these newer congregations in cities like Boston. They also seem to be emerging in historic congregations such as Park Street Church. While they don't always have the same "look" as the grand revivals of the past, they seem to be just as genuine—as longtime believers are spiritually refreshed and those who are outside the family of faith are transformed by God's amazing grace. Spiritual awakening, after all, is

---

Douglas Hall is President of Emmanuel Gospel Center and Rudy Mitchell is Senior Researcher. According to studies conducted by the Emmanuel Gospel Center, the number of Protestant churches in Boston has increased from 203 in 1981 to more than 412 in 2000. Over the past two decades, attendance grew from 15 to 800 at the Lion of Judah, a predominantly Spanish-speaking congregation; from 18 to 1000 at Boston's Chinese Evangelical Church; and from 60 to 5000 at the Jubilee Christian Church, a predominantly black congregation.

73. Edith L. Blumhofer and Randall Balmer, eds., *Modern Christian Revivals* (Urbana: University of Illinois Press, 1993); Philip Jenkins, *The Next Christendom: The Coming of Global Christianity* (New York: Oxford University Press, 2002); Lamin Sanneh, *Whose Religion Is Christianity? The Gospel Beyond the West* (Grand Rapids: Eerdmans, 2003); Allan Anderson, *An Introduction to Pentecostalism: Global Charismatic Christianity* (Cambridge: Cambridge University Press, 2004); Walter J. Hollenweger, *Pentecostalism: Origins and Developments Worldwide* (Peabody, MA: Hendrickson, 1997); Gary B. McGee, "Pentecostal Phenomena and Revivals in India," *International Bulletin of Missionary Research* 20, no. 3 (July 1, 1996): 112–17; Fred T. Corum, *Like as of Fire: Newspapers from the Azusa Street World Wide Revival* (Washington, DC: Middle Atlantic Regional Press, 1989); Robert Coleman, *The Coming World Revival: Your Part in God's Plan to Reach the World* (Wheaton, IL: Crossway, 1995); and Ajith Fernando, *Sharing the Truth in Love* (Grand Rapids: Discovery House, 2001).

74. Eddie Gibbs quoted in Jay Lindsay, "Greater Boston in Midst of a Quiet Religious Revival," *Boston Globe*, January 15, 2005.

never an end in itself. It simply prepares Christ's followers for the ministry God has called them to do. And that task includes the communication of the gospel by deeds as well as words.

c h a p t e r   f o u r

Engaging the Culture

A light rain was falling, that unseasonably chilly Fourth of July in 1829, as William Lloyd Garrison and a small group of his friends "set out to walk the six blocks uphill from their downtown rooming house for the four-o'clock lecture."[1] The young reformer, then largely unknown, had worked on his speech for more than a week. It would, he warned his friends, be "severe, long, and likely to give offense."[2] It would also help to establish him as one of the most prominent antislavery advocates in American history.

Despite the weather, a sizeable crowd had gathered at Park Street Church for the occasion. Garrison "felt his knees knock together," as historian Henry Mayer has reported, "at the thought of speaking before so large a concourse."[3] Heartened by the antislavery anthem performed by Park Street's choir, a presentation that Garrison found both "beautiful and thrilling," his fear soon gave way to the flinty resolve for which he is usually remembered.[4] Garrison, of

---

1. Henry Mayer, *All on Fire: William Lloyd Garrison and the Abolition of Slavery* (New York: St. Martin's Griffin, 1998), 63. For Mayer's account of Garrison's famous speech at Park Street Church, see pp. 44–70.
2. William Lloyd Garrison, "Address to the Colonization Society" (address, Park Street Church, Boston, Massachusetts, July 4, 1829).
3. Mayer, *All on Fire*, 62–68.
4. For the words of the antislavery anthem see Wendell Phillips Garrison and

course, was not the first antislavery speaker to occupy the Park
Street pulpit. Since 1823, in fact, during Sereno Dwight's pastorate, Park Street Church had been hosting a series of antislavery
addresses each July 4. The tradition, reflecting the strong reformist
impulse within evangelicalism, was continued by Dwight's successor, Edward Beecher—the son of Lyman Beecher and the brother
of Catherine Beecher (a pioneer in female education), Henry Ward
Beecher (the well-known preacher), and Harriet Beecher Stowe
(author of *Uncle Tom's Cabin*).[5] From its earliest years Park Street
had positioned itself at "the forefront of a movement designed to
hasten abolition, but in a peaceful and wise manner."[6]

The American Colonization Society, the official sponsor of the
gathering, had been established in 1816 to work toward the gradual
eradication of slavery in America and the establishment of a colony
in West Africa to which the freed slaves could return.[7] At the time
of his address in 1829, Garrison's own approach to the problem of
slavery was still essentially "gradualist." "Years may elapse," he told
the Park Street congregation, before slavery can be fully defeated.
"The fabric, which now towers above the Alps, must be taken away
brick by brick, and foot by foot, till it is reduced so low that it may
be overturned without burying the nation in its ruins." Yet, there
"must be a beginning, and now is a propitious time—perhaps the

Francis Jackson Garrison, *William Lloyd Garrison, 1805–1879: The Story of
His Life Told by His Children* (New York: Century Company, 1885), 1:126;
H. Crosby Englizian, *Brimstone Corner* (Chicago: Moody Press, 1968),
130–31; or Mayer, *All on Fire*, 63. For an example of antislavery words sung
to "America," see the Hingham Anti-Slavery Society's 1843 songbook,
included with the set of illustrations following p. 232 in Mayer, *All on Fire*.

5. Stephen H. Snyder, *Lyman Beecher and His Children* (Brooklyn, NY:
Carlson Publishers, 1991); and Samuel A. Schreiner, *The Passionate Beechers*
(Hoboken, NJ: John Wiley, 2003).

6. Englizian, *Brimstone Corner*, 129. For an excellent discussion of "The
Antislavery Upheaval," as he titled his chapter, and its relationship to the
history of Park Street Church, see pp. 125–35. A native New Englander,
Garrison was born on December 10, 1805, in the little house immediately next
door to Old South Presbyterian Church in Newburyport, Massachusetts—
the "Whitefield Church," as it has often been called because it is where the
famous Anglican preacher, George Whitefield, is buried.

7. Eric Burin, *Slavery and the Peculiar Solution: A History of the American
Colonization Society* (Gainesville: University of Florida Press, 2005).

last opportunity that will be granted us by a long-suffering God." Consequently, "I call upon the ambassadors of Christ everywhere to make known this proclamation: 'Thus saith the Lord God of the Africans, Let this people go, that they may serve me.' I ask them to 'proclaim liberty to the captives, and the opening of the prison to them that are bound'—to light up a flame of philanthropy that shall burn till all Africa be redeemed from the night of moral death, and the song of deliverance be heard throughout her borders. I call upon the churches of the living God to lead this great enterprise," Garrison exhorted. "Let them combine their energies, and systematize their plans, for the rescue of suffering humanity. Let them pour out their supplications to heaven in behalf of the slave. Prayer is omnipotent: its breath can melt adamantine rocks—its touch can break the stoutest chains." Therefore, he concluded, "let anti-slavery charity-boxes stand uppermost among those for missionary, tract and educational purposes. On this subject, Christians have been asleep; let them shake off their slumbers, and arm for the holy contest."[8]

Banner from the *Liberator,* date unknown. Courtesy of Park Street Church.

By the time he launched the *Liberator,* his famous Boston-based antislavery newspaper, in 1831, however, it was clear that Garrison had abandoned the society's "gradualist" strategy. "I will be as harsh as truth, and as uncompromising as justice," he wrote in his first editorial, for "I do not wish to think, or to speak, or write, with moderation. No! No! Tell a man whose house is on fire to give a moderate alarm; tell him to moderately rescue his wife from the hands of the ravisher; tell the mother to gradually extricate her

---

8. Garrison, "Address to the Colonization Society," 5–6.

babe from the fire into which it has fallen;—but urge me not to use moderation in a cause like the present." Therefore, Garrison concluded, "I will not equivocate—I will not excuse—I will not retreat a single inch—AND I WILL BE HEARD. The apathy of the people is enough to make every statue leap from its pedestal, and to hasten the resurrection of the dead."[9]

Although most of Park Street's members were sympathetic with the antislavery cause, few seemed prepared to adopt Garrison's increasingly radical positions on how this important goal should be achieved. Some feared that the abandonment of the American Colonization Society's gradual emancipation strategy by abolitionists like Garrison—combined with their increasingly strident call for immediate emancipation—could produce unnecessary bloodshed and might even do irreparable damage to the overall cause. While Park Street's building continued to be used throughout the 1830s for meetings of both the American Colonization Society and the New England Antislavery Society, its membership—like the Boston community itself—was becoming increasingly divided over matters of strategy.[10]

Evangelicalism's Forgotten Roots

Such divisions, however, should not be allowed to obscure the profoundly reformist roots of the evangelical movement.[11] During the first half of the nineteenth century, as historian Donald W. Dayton has demonstrated, evangelicalism had "reverberated with vitality and reform activity."[12] Indeed, literally thousands of evangelical Christians, determined to apply the teaching of the Bible in every aspect of life and work, became actively involved in everything

---

9. William Lloyd Garrison, "To the Public," *Liberator*, January 1, 1831. See also William Lloyd Garrison, *Thoughts on African Colonization* (Boston: Garrison & Knapp, 1832).

10. Bertram Wyatt-Brown, *Lewis Tappan and the Evangelical War Against Slavery* (Cleveland: Case Western Reserve University, 1969).

11. See Timothy L. Smith, *Revivalism and Social Reform: American Protestantism on the Eve of the Civil War* (Eugene, OR: Wipf & Stock, 2005); and Norris Magnuson, *Salvation in the Slums* (Eugene, OR: Wipf & Stock, 2005).

12. Donald W. Dayton, *Discovering an Evangelical Heritage* (New York: Harper & Row, 1976), 5.

from antislavery and prison reform to temperance, poverty relief, and women's rights. Whether one is speaking of the great evangelical revivals that swept across the British Isles during the era of the Wesleys, George Whitefield, and William Wilberforce or across North America during the Second Great Awakening, a fundamental linkage between biblical Christianity and social reform is clearly visible.[13]

Evangelicalism's most prominent American voice, for example, was an outspoken opponent of slavery. Having been invited by Park Street Church to come for a series of meetings in 1832, and again in 1843 and 1857, the reformist views of evangelist Charles G. Finney were well known to the congregation. "Revivals are hindered," Finney often remarked, "when ministers and *churches take wrong ground in regard to any question involving human rights.*" Make no mistake about it, Finney argued, this "abominable abomination" we know as *slavery* is nothing less than a sin against almighty God— and it is time that "this monster is dragged from his horrid den, and exhibited before the church" and called "by its true name." Indeed, "the time has come, in the providence of God, when every southern breeze is loaded down with the cries of lamentation, mourning and woe." More than two million in our own land "stretch their hands, all shackled and bleeding, and send forth to the church of God the agonizing cry for help. And shall the church, in her efforts to reclaim and save the world, deafen her ears to this voice of agony and despair? God forbid. The church cannot turn away from this question," Finney reminded his listeners, for "it is a question for the church and for the nation to decide, and God will push it to a decision." Our "silence can no longer be accounted for upon the principle of ignorance"— and we can no longer remain "silent without guilt."[14]

---

13. Garth M. Rosell, "Charles G. Finney: His Place in the Stream of American Evangelicalism," in *The Evangelical Tradition in America*, ed. Leonard I. Sweet (Macon, GA: Mercer University Press, 1997), 131–47. See also Leon O. Hynson, *To Reform the Nation* (Grand Rapids: Zondervan, 1984); and Kevin Belmonte, *Hero for Humanity: A Biography of William Wilberforce* (Colorado Springs, CO: NavPress, 2002).
14. Charles G. Finney, *Lectures on Revivals of Religion*, ed. William G. McLoughlin Jr. (1835; repr., Cambridge, MA: Belknap Press of Harvard University Press, 1960), 287–88.

Although the church's primary task must always be evangelism, Finney was sure, the application of biblical truth to issues of social justice was not simply an optional exercise. Indeed, when great matters of social justice are neglected, he believed, the Christian community both dishonors God and thwarts the work of revival. Therefore, revival and reform must always be linked together, Finney believed, and pastors must be trained in such a manner as to pursue both of these important tasks. The establishment of Oberlin Collegiate Institute in 1833, an institution that Finney served as president for a time and at which he taught for many years, became a kind of educational laboratory for training precisely that kind of leadership.[15] As the first college in America to admit both women and African American students, Oberlin sought to reflect in its institutional practice what Finney had been proclaiming from the pulpit—and in so doing, to borrow the words of historian Gilbert H. Barnes, "released a mighty impulse toward social reform."[16]

Lyman Beecher, whose own connections with Park Street Church we have already explored, had accepted an appointment as president of Lane Seminary and pastor of Second Presbyterian Church in Cincinnati in 1832.[17] "Beecher's brand of reform," as Dayton explains, "was more moderate and 'polite'" than was Finney's. As to the slavery issue, Beecher "was committed to gradual abolition and colonization," reflecting a position similar to that of the American Colonization Society, deeming slavery as "wrong" but stopping short of labeling it as a "sin."[18] Finney and Oberlin, on the

15. Garth M. Rosell, "A Speckled Bird: Charles G. Finney's Contribution to Higher Education," *Fides et Historia*, Summer 1993, 55–74. The standard history of Oberlin College is Robert Samuel Fletcher, *A History of Oberlin College: From Its Foundation Through the Civil War*, 2 vols. (Oberlin, OH: Oberlin College, 1943). Finney began his teaching at Oberlin in 1835 and became its president in 1850.

16. Gilbert Hobbs Barnes, *The Anti-Slavery Impulse: 1830–1844* (New York: Harcourt, Brace and World, 1964), 11.

17. Lyman Beecher, as we have seen, had preached the ordination service for Sereno Dwight and the five missionary candidates in 1817, had served as pastor of Boston's Hanover Street Church from 1826 to 1832, and had observed with fatherly pleasure the appointment of his own son Edward to the pastorate at Park Street Church (a position he held from 1826 to 1830).

18. Dayton, *Discovering an Evangelical Heritage*, 35.

other hand, did not hesitate to call slavery a great national sin—an abomination that was doing irreparable harm to the nation as well as the church. Consequently, with the establishment of Oberlin Collegiate Institute, virtually the entire Lane Seminary student body, including the great antislavery reformer Theodore Dwight Weld, left Lane Seminary in Cincinnati to enroll as students at Oberlin. While there, as Finney described it in his *Memoirs*, they discovered a community that sought to combine the great tasks of revival and reform, to train women as well as men with what they called "the right kind of education," and to make "no distinction on account of color."[19]

Although virtually all of Park Street's members were opposed to slavery, most rejected the increasingly radical positions espoused by William Lloyd Garrison. They remained divided, however, with regard to how the problem should be handled. While some were willing to follow Finney and his Oberlin colleagues, others were more comfortable with Beecher's gradualist approach. In this respect, among others, Park Street's members were simply reflecting in microcosm the terrible struggles that would eventually divide families, congregations, and an entire nation. Great social issues seldom yield to easy solutions. To simply ignore them, however, as our nineteenth-century brothers and sisters would quickly remind us, can bring disastrous and costly results.

The Benevolent Empire

There can be little question that slavery was the defining moral issue of antebellum America. It was not, however, the only concern that captured the attention of the church. Indeed, during the first half of the nineteenth century, as historian Donald Mathews has suggested, a "general social movement" seems to have been in progress, organizing "thousands of people into small groups." Established to "change the moral character of America," these societies were

19. Garth M. Rosell and Richard A. G. Dupuis, eds., *The Memoirs of Charles G. Finney: The Complete Restored Text* (Grand Rapids: Zondervan, 1989), 411. For an excellent discussion of the "Lane Rebellion" and the beginnings of Oberlin see Dayton, *Discovering an Evangelical Heritage*, 35–62.

able to mobilize "Americans in unprecedented numbers."[20] Known generally as "the benevolent empire," a number of large national organizations and literally hundreds of small local committees joined hands in an effort to reform the prisons, feed the hungry, distribute Bibles and tracts, promote missionary outreach, end the slave trade, widen educational opportunities, lobby legislators for humane and godly laws, fight the abuses of alcohol, work for peace, take care of the families of injured stage coach drivers, care for the sick, look after the orphans, and participate in additional causes as well. Societies were even formed with the single purpose of praying for the success of all the other societies.[21] "What a fertility of projects," exclaimed Ralph Waldo Emerson, "for the salvation of the world."[22]

Many of the members of Park Street Church, like those in other evangelical congregations, became passionately engaged in these reformist efforts. It is not by chance, after all, that the American Education Society, the Sandwich Islands Church, the Park Street Singing Society (a forerunner of the Handel and Haydn Society), the Boston chapter of the NAACP, the Animal Rescue League, the Prison Discipline Society, and the American Temperance Society, to name some of the more prominent groups, were all established at Park Street Church. Neither should it come as a surprise to discover that the annual gatherings of some of these societies—and others such as the New England Antislavery Society and the American Colonization Society—were held in Park Street's beautiful sanctuary on the Boston Common. Nor should we wonder why Park Street's doors were opened to speakers like William Lloyd Garrison and Charles Sumner, whose now-famous address, "The War System of the Commonwealth of Nations," was delivered on May 28, 1849,

---

20. Donald G. Mathews, "The Second Great Awakening as an Organizing Process, 1790–1830: An Hypothesis," in *The American Quarterly* 22 (Spring 1969): 27, 30–31, 35. See also Lefferts A. Loetscher, "The Problem of Christian Unity in Early 19th Century America," in *Church History* 32 (March 1963): 3–16.
21. For a fuller discussion of this movement see Rosell, "Charles G. Finney," 140–47.
22. Ralph Waldo Emerson, *Essays* (Boston: Ticknor and Fields, 1867), 243.

from Park Street's pulpit.[23] After all, throughout much of the nineteenth century, evangelical Christians—and evangelical churches like Park Street—were at the center of a massive crusade to address injustice and to promote biblical Christianity.

"The moral enterprises of the present day are novel," wrote one newspaper editor, not so much "in their character and principle" as "in their combination and effect." What a joy it will be "for our country and the world," he mused, if future generations can exclaim: "These were the men of the nineteenth century, who came to the help of the Lord against the mighty;—these defenders of the sabbath and all its holy influences;—these friends and patrons of missionary and Bible institutions;—these supporters of a press truly free, which, by its salutary issues, emancipated the nation from the thraldom of sin;—these are the men who counted the cost of denying themselves and cheerfully made effort for the world's deliverance. God smiled upon their persevering and united labors," he concluded, "acknowledged them as his friends and servants, and we now hail them as benefactors of our happy millions, and thousands of millions yet unborn."[24]

The Great Reversal

Given the "benevolent empire's" historic commitment to social justice, as reflected in the early decades of Park Street's own history, one is tempted to wonder about what might have happened to the reforming spirit within the evangelical movement. The answer, of course, "is complex and perhaps can never be completely explained."[25] In his response to the question, however, sociologist David Moberg offers "the Great Reversal" as a possible

---

23. A copy of Charles Sumner, "The War System of the Commonwealth of Nations," delivered at Park Street Church on May 28, 1849, can be found at the Boston Athanaeum.

24. Albert G. Hall, ed., *Rochester Observer*, March 12, 1830.

25. Dayton responds to this question in his chapter, "What Ever Happened to Evangelicalism?" in *Discovering an Evangelical Heritage*, 121–35. For the classic discussion of the "Great Reversal," as Timothy L. Smith labeled it, see David O. Moberg, *The Great Reversal: Evangelism and Social Concern* (Philadelphia and New York: J. B. Lippincott, 1972).

explanation. Since the early decades of the twentieth century, he observed, American Christians have been divided "into two camps"—namely, the "soul-winners" (the fundamentalist wing) and the "social gospelers" (the modernist or ecumenical wing).[26] Polarized by the profound religious debates that reached their peak in the 1920s, called by many historians the "fundamentalist-modernist controversy," the fundamentalists increasingly turned inward, focused on personal evangelism, and withdrew in the process from scores of institutions that they believed had fallen into the hands of the liberals. The modernists, meanwhile, increasingly defined their task as that of "redeeming the social order."[27] As a result—although it may well have been a classic case of unintended consequences—many evangelical Christians, wishing to remain true to the fundamental teachings of the Bible, found that they had also abandoned their historic commitment to social reform.

Reversing the Great Reversal

Among the leading voices of those seeking to reverse this Great Reversal during the 1940s and 1950s was the twelfth pastor of Park Street Church.[28] "The evangelical defense of the faith theologically," Harold John Ockenga insisted, "is identical with that of the older fundamentalists." Evangelicals and fundamentalists differ, however, on matters of strategy. Ockenga and many of his colleagues believed that the evangelical movement must abandon its propensity to withdraw from the culture and its institutions and commit itself rather to the "principle of infiltration." Evangelicals "need to realize that the liberals, or modernists, have been using this strategy for years. They have infiltrated our evangelical denominations, institutions and movements," Ockenga was convinced, "and they

---

26. For his complete argument, see Moberg, *The Great Reversal.*

27. For the best discussion of the fundamentalist controversy, see George M. Marsden, *Fundamentalism and American Culture: The Shaping of Twentieth-Century Evangelicalism: 1870–1925* (New York: Oxford University Press, 1980).

28. See Garth M. Rosell, *The Surprising Work of God: Harold John Ockenga, Billy Graham and the Rebirth of Evangelicalism* (Grand Rapids: Baker, 2008).

have taken over control of them." Ockenga called evangelicals to "infiltrate" those same structures with the salt and light of biblical Christianity.[29]

David Moberg has suggested that "the first prominent spokesman calling for a revival of interest in social issues" was Ockenga's old friend, Carl Henry. Calling for a "new reformation," Henry's *Uneasy Conscience of Modern Fundamentalism* spelled out "the implications of personal regeneration for social as well as individual problems."[30] Most evangelical ministers, "during the past generation of world disintegration," Henry observed, "became increasingly less vocal about social evils." Henry once asked a group of more than one hundred evangelical pastors how many of them over the course of the past six months had "preached a sermon devoted in large part to a condemnation of such social evils as aggressive warfare, racial hatred and intolerance, the liquor traffic, exploitation of labor or management, or the like." "Not a single hand," he reported, "was raised in response."[31]

Unlike those evangelical pastors, Harold John Ockenga had preached numerous times on every one of the issues on Henry's list: from racial hatred and intolerance, to exploitation of labor, the liquor traffic, aggressive warfare, and many more besides. As early as the fall of 1934, for example, Ockenga preached a series of sermons on social issues—including a strong condemnation of racial prejudice—at the Point Breeze Presbyterian Church in Pittsburgh. After coming to Park Street Church in 1936, he continued to address from the Boston pulpit a wide range of social

---

29. Harold John Ockenga, "Resurgent Evangelical Leadership," in *Christianity Today*, October 10, 1960, 11–15. In his influential book, *Christ and Culture*, H. Richard Niebuhr suggested that at least five different "types," or "zones" as historian Martin Marty prefers to call them, have characterized Christianity's understanding of the relation between the church and culture throughout its history. While all five of these can be found, often in overlapping configurations, within evangelicalism, Harold John Ockenga's "principle of infiltration" seems at first glance to fit most easily into the fifth: Christ the Transformer of Culture.

30. Moberg, *The Great Reversal*, 160.

31. Carl F. H. Henry, *The Uneasy Conscience of Modern Fundamentalism* (Grand Rapids: Eerdmans, 1947), 4.

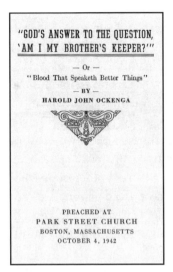

"GOD'S ANSWER TO THE QUESTION,
'AM I MY BROTHER'S KEEPER?'"

— Or —
"Blood That Speaketh Better Things"

— BY —
HAROLD JOHN OCKENGA

PREACHED AT
PARK STREET CHURCH
BOSTON, MASSACHUSETTS
OCTOBER 4, 1942

Printed sermon pamphlet by Harold John Ockenga, October 4, 1942. Courtesy of Gordon-Conwell Libraries.

issues such as poverty, racism, exploitation of labor, alcoholism, and many others.[32]

"God hears the cry of the suffering," Ockenga reminded his Park Street congregation in 1942. "God hears the whimpering of a lost and hungry child orphaned in China, the sobbing of some poor mother, the groaning of a bayoneted man," he continued, "just as much as He hears the sobbing of your beautiful little child who may be orphaned through this war. God is no respecter of persons." The problem, Ockenga explained, is that people continue to follow the rebellious path of Cain rather than the righteous path of Abel. "Am I my brother's keeper?" Cain asked. "Shall I let the world rot in its corruption? Shall I let it stew in its envy, its hate, its greed, its malice, its brutality, its violence and its festering social sores?" What is that to the church? Yet, the "blood of the murdered Abel" cries out

---

32. See, for example, "God and the Depression" (April 17, 1932); "Race Prejudice" (October 14, 1934); "God's Answer to the Question, 'Am I My Brother's Keeper?'" (October 4, 1942); "The Solution to the Social Question" (October 10, 1943); plus a number of undated sermons such as "Humanitarian Religion," "War—Are We Dupes of the Munition Makers?" "America's Great Menace [alcohol]," "God and the Struggle for Bread," "The Church's Attitude Toward Work," and "Crime." Manuscript copies of these sermons can be found in the Ockenga Papers.

"from the ground unto God for judgment and vengeance against him who shed it"—and "unquestionably the blood of millions of innocent ones cries from the ground against us."[33]

"The way of Cain is the way of death." It has no room "for the Christ of Calvary," no room "for the humanitarianism inspired by Christ," no room "for the world missionary vision and for the desire to enlighten those who sit in darkness and in the shadow of death." On the contrary, it fosters only "selfishness, envy, hate, violence and evil" and it divides brother from brother, sons from parents, creatures from their creator, nation from nation, and race from race. On the other hand, the blood of Christ "unites." Indeed, it was Christ's atoning work on the cross "that binds us into a unit. By it we are bound to God, to Christ and to each other. Our fellowship is with the Father and with his son Jesus Christ." Nothing within the universe has the capacity to "bind closer, more securely and more permanently than this covenant blood. Nothing is more calculated to put an end to the hideous theories of race and blood and violence in the world today than the precious unity of man in the blood of Christ." And it is because of this unity in Christ "that we begin to understand our union with mankind" and the grave responsibilities that this fundamental unity places upon all of us. "Hence in Calvary and what Christ has done for us," Ockenga concluded, Christians discover that we are indeed our brother's keeper. We "can do nothing to a man without doing it to Christ who assumed human flesh." If we "treat humanity with indignity, violence and brutality," we "are doing it to Christ." And that we cannot do "for in Him we realize our racial unity. This is the source of our ethics."[34]

---

33. Ockenga used the 150th anniversary of William Carey's famous speech to preach from Genesis 4, asking his congregation, "Am I My Brother's Keeper?" Representatives of the American Board of Commissioners for Foreign Missions were also in attendance on that occasion. Carey's address (including the well-known line "Expect great things from God; Attempt great things for God") was delivered on October 2, 1792, to the Baptist Ministers Meeting in Kettering. It is considered by many to mark the beginning of the modern missionary movement.
34. Ockenga, "Am I My Brother's Keeper?"

Ockenga's convictions about racial injustice, while perhaps unusual for the historical period in which he lived, would hardly have sounded strange to his evangelical heroes, Charles G. Finney (whom he considered "America's Greatest Revivalist")[35] and John Wesley (whose theology he had learned at his mother's knee).[36] Wesley for example, had "attacked slavery as a contradiction of humanity, reason, and natural law."[37] Do not "be weary of well doing," Wesley had written in a letter to William Wilberforce, the great evangelical antislavery voice in the British Parliament, supporting his efforts to bring an end to the slave trade throughout the British Empire. "Go on, in the name of God and in the power of his might, till even American slavery (the vilest that ever saw the sun) shall vanish away before it." Then referring to a tract he had just read that morning by "a poor African," Wesley continued, "I was particularly struck by that circumstance that a man who has a black skin, being wronged or outraged by a white man, can have no redress; it being a 'law' in all our colonies that the *oath* of a black against a white goes for nothing. What villainy is this?"[38]

Ockenga was well aware of Wesley's writings on the subject of slavery. In a 1934 sermon that he preached on the problem of racism, in fact, he seems to draw special inspiration from Wesley's 1774 tract, *Thoughts upon Slavery*. It is God's intention, Wesley had argued, that "every child of man," indeed "every partaker of human nature," should enjoy the benefits of liberty. "Let none serve you," he wrote, "but by his own act and deed, by his own voluntary choice." So "away with all whips, all chains, all compulsion! Be gentle toward all men. And see that you invariably do unto every one, as you would he should do unto *You*." Since it is God, Wesley was convinced, "who hast mingled of one blood, all the nations

---

35. Harold John Ockenga, "The Secret of America's Greatest Revivalist" (sermon, Park Street Church, 1937), Ockenga Papers.
36. See Harold John Ockenga, "The Warmed Heart of John Wesley and Methodism" (undated sermon, Park Street Church), Ockenga Papers.
37. Hynson, *To Reform the Nation*, 49.
38. Letter from John Wesley to William Wilberforce (February 24, 1791) in *John Wesley*, ed. Albert C. Outler (New York: Oxford University Press, 1980), 85–86.

upon earth," it is the church's obligation to place itself clearly on the side of mercy, justice, and truth.[39]

Following the lead of theological mentors such as Wesley and Finney, Ockenga found the answers to these great social questions in Scripture. "God has not left us without guidance," he declared, but has "given us principles" by which to solve our problems. In all human relationships, be they parent and child, husband and wife, or employer and employee, God regards each party—"the great or the small," the "servant or master," the "black or white," the "male or female"—with exactly the same care and concern. "There is no respect of persons with God," Ockenga declared. "There is no difference out of Christ," for all are sinners in need of salvation. "There is no difference in Christ," for all are "Christians and children of God." Consequently, from the divine perspective, all individuals are both free and equal.

What would happen to employer-employee relations, race consciousness, social inequality and injustices, and class conflicts, Ockenga asked, if people were to gather at the foot of the cross? The result, Ockenga was convinced, would be the overthrow of "exploitation, injustice, and oppression." True Christianity begins "with our vertical relationship to God" but it must always include our "horizontal relationship with men." Since "what we do to men, we do to God," God will hold us "responsible for our deeds." "Christianity is the most practical element in life," Ockenga concluded. "Embrace Christ and the crux of the social question is removed."[40]

Engaging the Culture: Preaching, Music, and the Arts

Park Street Church "has been engaged in humanitarian activities from the very beginning," observed Harold John Ockenga in 1961. "It has borne its testimony in the anti-slavery movement, in the prison reform movement, in the founding of the Animal Rescue League, in the Watch and Ward Society, in the National

---

39. John Wesley, *Thoughts upon Slavery* (London: R. Hawes, 1774), 29–53.
40. Ockenga, "The Solution to the Social Problem."

Association of Evangelicals and many other humanitarian and societal movements."[41] It has also, he might have added, sought to give witness to the glorious gospel through its ministries of preaching, music, and the arts.

Following the evening service on May 30, 1943, for example, Ockenga had the sextons set up an old table, adjacent to the church but overlooking the Boston Common. Since the congregation had unsuccessfully petitioned the Park Department for permission to use the Parkman Bandstand on the Common for the service, they were forced to employ a somewhat makeshift arrangement. The results were striking. "Last Sunday night at 9:00 PM," a notice in the church bulletin for June 6 reported, "over 3,500 people gathered on the Lafayette Mall for our Singspiration and to hear Dr. Ockenga preach. The mighty bell rang for fifteen minutes and a capacity congregation poured out from the church to mingle with hundreds who had been on the mall listening to the broadcast of the sermon preached in the church. Thousands of others immediately joined the crowd to see what was happening." The following week, at the urging of the Park Department, a permit was granted by the Mayor's Office, and the gathering was held at the Parkman Bandstand. Throughout the summer, each Sunday evening at 9:00 PM, "a singspiration and preaching service" were held at the bandstand—with between three thousand and ten thousand in attendance at each service. As a result of these gatherings, according to the reports, many "responded to the invitation to accept Christ."[42]

When Park Street's request to renew the permit in 1945 was denied, as the result of objections that had been raised "by certain religious interests in the city," one of Park Street's members offered to donate sufficient funds to construct what came to be known as the Mayflower Pulpit, and to provide funding for the construction and furnishing of the Mayflower Room as well as "the amplification

---

41. Harold John Ockenga, "News Release," Monday, January 2, 1961, 2. Manuscript copy in the Park Street archives.
42. The quotations are taken from "The History of the Mayflower Pulpit," a three-page typed manuscript in the Park Street Church archives, author unknown.

facilities" that would be needed. The Mayflower Pulpit was officially dedicated on June 2, 1946 and immediately "put to use for the preaching of the Gospel." For many years from June through September, weather permitting, the gospel was proclaimed each week from that location.

The "Mayflower Pulpit" on the 125th anniversary of the first singing of "America," June 30, 1956. Courtesy of Park Street Church.

Park Street's efforts to reach the community through preaching were greatly strengthened through its well-known ministry of music. On January 17, 1810, the week following the dedication of the new sanctuary, the Park Street Singing Society was formed at the home of Caleb Bingham. "Their aim," as Englizian has noted, "was to introduce tunes of a more sacred quality and the plain and solemn music of the masters in place of the light, fuguing melodies common to the churches of the day." The music was of such a high quality, in fact, that it not only "attracted large numbers of Bostonians" to Park Street's regular services but it also spawned the establishment of America's oldest oratorio society in 1815, the Handel and Haydn Society.[43]

It was the arrival of Lowell Mason and his wife, however, that put Park Street on the musical map.[44] While working as a bank clerk in Savannah, Georgia, he had become widely known throughout the region as a fine organist and musician. He had also served as the superintendent of the Sunday school at First Presbyterian Church in that city, a congregation pastored by Henry Kollock. It was through Dr. Kollock, in fact, that his musical abilities became known to the "committee of churchmen" in Boston. This led, in due time, to an invitation for Mason to come to Boston for the purpose of establishing "singing schools" and to help "elevate church music generally throughout the city."[45] When he arrived in 1827, he worked as a bank clerk; established "several private and church-related schools of music," one of which met in Park Street's vestry; and accepted an appointment as "choirmaster and organist" at Park Street Church. While his tenure at Park Street was relatively brief, extending from 1829 to 1831, his impact on the congregation and the city of Boston was immense. It was Mason who took the patriotic words of a young Andover Theological Seminary student named Samuel F. Smith and performed "America" for the very first time at a July 4, 1831, service at Park Street Church.[46] It was

43. Englizian, *Brimstone Corner,* 114. I am indebted to H. Crosby Englizian for his excellent discussion of the importance of music in Park Street's history. See his chapter on "Sacred Music and Sabbath Education," pp. 113–24. See also the preface to *The Boston Handel and Haydn Society Collection of Church Music; Being a Selection of the Most Approved Psalm and Hymn Tunes; Together with Many Beautiful Extracts from the Work of Haydn, Mozart, Beethoven, and Other Eminent Modern Composers,* 5th ed. (Boston: Richardson and Lord, 1827), 1–3.

44. Lowell Mason (1792–1872), the famous organist, music educator, composer, hymn writer, and bank clerk, was born in Medfield, Massachusetts. Trained in Europe, he is credited with having an important role in bringing music education to Boston's schools. His collections of hymns and anthems sold over a million copies. See Carol A. Pemberton, *Lowell Mason: His Life and Work* (Ann Arbor, MI: UMI Research Press, 1985); and Michael Broyles, ed., *Yankee Musician in Europe: The 1837 Journals of Lowell Mason* (Rochester, NY: University of Rochester Press, 1996).

45. Englizian, *Brimstone Corner,* 116.

46. For the correct dating of the first public performance see the letters of Henry

Mason who took the lyrics of Ray Palmer, a young man who had
come to faith in Christ at Park Street Church, and added the music
for "My Faith Looks Up to Thee." And it was Mason who left the
Christian churches with scores of hymns—from "When I Survey
the Wondrous Cross" to "Nearer My God to Thee"—treasures that
continue to be used in Park Street's services to this very day. For
more than half a century, Mason remained the "dominant personality" in shaping "the philosophy and instruction of church and
school music." His collections of hymns and anthems sold more
than a million copies.[47]

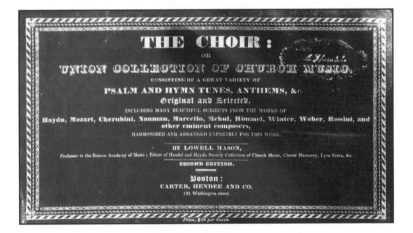

Title page of *The Choir*. Courtesy of Park Street Church.

Mason believed that the purpose of church music was "to attract
and fix the attention, to excite and express religious emotions and,

Lowell Mason to Ralph C. Fitts (June 18, 1957) and Ralph C. Fitts to the Hon.
Henry Lowell Mason (on Park Street Church stationery, no date) in the Park
Street Church archives. For the story of how Samuel Smith came to write
his famous song see Nelson G. Morton, "No Thought of a National Hymn
When Dr. Smith Wrote 'America,'" *Boston Sunday Globe*, February 14, 1931.

47. Mason would probably have remained at Park Street had it not been that
Lyman Beecher's Hanover Street Church made him a better offer: a larger
seating area for the choir, a better organ, and "the prospect of introducing
his own hymnal into the church." See Englizian, *Brimstone Corner*, 119. A
copy of Lowell Mason's *The Choir: or Union Collection of Church Music* can
be found in the Park Street Church archives.

through its union with language, to excite and express religious sentiments." It was not simply a preparation for worship; it was an essential part of worship. Consequently, the "choir should lead in music," the direction should come from "a competent master," and the music should be "accompanied by an organ."[48] Mason's philosophy, to a remarkable degree, continues to guide the services of worship at Park Street to this very day under the superb leadership of Park Street's codirectors of music, C. Thomas Brooks and Robert Bloodworth, and its outstanding organist, Roy Brunner. While a broader range of musical styles and instrumentation have been introduced as a regular part of the evening services, reflecting some of the more contemporary trends in Christian music, Mason's passion for excellence has remained a priority throughout the church at every one of its services.

Since the days of Lowell Mason, Park Street Church has been served by four organs (and a number of outstanding organists and choir directors): the first organ was installed during Mason's tenure, the second in 1885, the third in 1910, and the current organ in 1961. The dedication of the Albert O. Wilson Memorial Organ and Cathedral Chimes in 1961, built by the Aeolian-Skinner Organ Company and the Maas-Rowe Company respectively, was marked with a gala recital by the well-known organist Virgil Fox. The three-manual console, controlling all five divisions of the organ, has seventy-five draw knobs, twenty-six couplers, and forty-eight combination pistons and pedals controlling more than three thousand pipes. It remains to this day a remarkable instrument.

Along with its preaching and music, Park Street has also sought to engage the community through the arts. Given the congregation's Puritan roots, with their strongly iconoclastic propensities, however, this has not always been an easy task.[49] "Classical

---

48. Englizian, *Brimstone Corner*, 118.
49. For the classic debates over the proper role of the arts in Christian worship, see the documents and discussion from the Seventh Ecumenical Council held in Nicaea in 787 in *A Select Library of Nicene and Post-Nicene Fathers of the Christian Church*, ed. Philip Schaff and Henry Wace, 2nd series, vol. 14, *The Seven Ecumenical Councils* (Grand Rapids: Eerdmans, 1971), 549–87; and John of Damascus, *On the Divine Images: Three Apologies Against Those*

Puritan worship on both sides of the Atlantic," as Horton Davies has argued, "was marked by a simplicity sometimes amounting to austerity." In their meetinghouses, there were "no stained-glass windows, no carved saints in niches, no rood screens," no paintings of the crucified Christ, "no brilliantly embossed ceilings, no beguiling organ music," and no "processions, bowings, crossings, or other gestures." There was a pulpit, to be sure, from which the Word of God was to be proclaimed—but in virtually every other respect, as Davies observed, the Puritans sought to maintain "the most economical simplicity imaginable."[50]

Consequently, throughout much of its history, Park Street Church has tended to approach the arts with caution. Like the Puritans before them, many have believed that the potential dangers of idolatry significantly outweigh the spiritual benefits that might come from such activities. The founders had an eye for beauty, to be sure, as evidenced in Park Street's magnificent building with its soaring steeple. Yet, many years were to pass before the congregation seemed ready to embrace the arts as a central part of its life and ministry.

The desire to avoid idolatry remains as strong as ever, yet a new appreciation for the arts has been emerging within the congregation—stimulated in part by the *Conference on Christianity in the Arts* that was held at Park Street Church in March of 1982. "The purpose of having this conference at Park Street Church is twofold," observed Paul E. Toms, the senior minister, namely "to celebrate Our Saviour as the agent of all creation and creativity, and to expand our influence in the world through all art forms. If the motive for our creativity is *soli Deo gloria*, our art will effectively ennoble those who experience it. So," he concluded, "we meet in conference for mutual learning, encouragement, and inspiration."[51]

Who Attack the Divine Images (Crestwood, NY: St. Vladimir's Seminary Press, 1980).

50. Horton Davies, *The Worship of the American Puritans* (Morgan, PA: Soli Deo Gloria Publications, 1999), 326–27. See also Leland Ryken, *Worldly Saints: The Puritans as They Really Were* (Grand Rapids: Zondervan, 1986), 111–36.

51. Paul E. Toms, in the program for the Conference on Christianity in the

The program, which included an array of impressive speakers, chamber concerts, art exhibitions, readings, and a series of workshops on music, writing, liturgical dance, drama, and the visual arts, served to highlight the importance of the arts within the life of the Christian community. While Park Street Church has served throughout its history as a venue for concerts, recitals, and lecture series, the conference helped to bring focused attention to the arts. These efforts have been continued and enlarged through the congregation's involvement in community events such as *First Night*, Boston's annual citywide celebration of the New Year, its extensive and respected music program, and the work of such ministries as *Soli Deo Gloria*.

Perhaps the most vivid illustration of the power of the arts when combined with the spoken word, however, came with the series of sermons preached by Park Street's fifteenth pastor, Gordon Hugenberger, on God's testing of Abraham in Genesis 22. In addition to the word pictures that were drawn from the pulpit, a visual depiction of Abraham's offering of his son Isaac was also provided through the artistic portrayal of the text by Bruce Herman. The combination of the two was absolutely electric—opening fresh insights into a difficult biblical text and deepening the congregation's understanding of the cost of obedience.

Salt and Light

"What kind of church should we be in the twenty-first century?" asked David C. Fisher in 1993. "We are a people bound by *Holy Scripture*," to be sure, but one that is obligated to apply that Word to its own "time and place."[52] He had reminded the congregation in a 1992 sermon that during the "Great Retreat" of the 1920s, evangelical Christianity "chose to be invisible." Then in the late 1940s, a group of Christian leaders, including Carl F. H. Henry and Billy Graham, "decided that the Great Retreat was wrong and something

---

Arts, March 5–7, 1982, at Park Street Church, Boston, Park Street Church archives.
52. David C. Fisher, "A Church for the Third Millennium" (sermon, Park Street Church, January 10, 1993), Park Street Church archives.

needed to be done." The "leader of the new movement was the pastor of this church, Dr. Harold Ockenga. In 1960, Ockenga wrote
an article in *Christianity Today* that proved to be prophetic"; he
observed that a "new generation of Christians" is emerging, a generation that is determined to affirm the importance of both "social
involvement" and "personal salvation." Seeking to reverse the
Great Reversal, as Timothy Smith had labeled evangelicalism's earlier withdrawal from culture, this movement challenges us "to get
out and make a difference in the church and our world."[53]

David C. Fisher, fourteenth pastor
of Park Street Church. Picture at
Park Street Church; photograph
by the author.

"There is not a square inch in the whole domain of our human
existence," Abraham Kuyper had observed in his inaugural address
at the Free University of Amsterdam, "over which Christ, who is
Sovereign over *all*, does not cry: 'Mine!'"[54] The implications of such
a grand vision are staggering. As followers of Christ, the church has
been commissioned to "go and make disciples of all nations, baptizing them in the name of the Father and of the Son and of the Holy
Spirit, and teaching them to obey everything I have commanded

53. David C. Fisher, "More Salt and Light" (sermon, Park Street Church,
    January 12, 1992), Park Street Church archives.
54. Abraham Kuyper, "Sphere Sovereignty," in *Abraham Kuyper: A Centennial
    Reader*, ed. James D. Bratt (Grand Rapids: Eerdmans, 1998), 488.

you. And surely I am with you always, to the very end of the age."[55] This Great Commission, Harold John Ockenga liked to remind his Park Street parishioners, includes not only "the worldwide evangelistic task," but also "the responsibility for moral reform and the sharing of humanitarian action." And it also involves, Ockenga never failed to add, the essential work of "Christian education."[56]

55. Matthew 28:19–20.
56. Harold John Ockenga, "The Foundations of Park Street Church,"(sermon, February 22, 1959, on the occasion of the congregation's 150th anniversary), Ockenga Papers.

c h a p t e r   f i v e

Renewing the Mind

B oston," wrote Oliver Wendell Holmes in 1858, "is the hub of the
solar system"—the center, by implication, of the intellectual universe.[1] Such a boastful claim, tongue-in-cheek to be sure, does con-
tain an element of truth. After all, within the Greater Boston region
there are scores of colleges and universities, nine theological seminaries, several music conservatories and schools of art, dozens of tech-
nical and professional schools, nearly one hundred fifty public grade
schools, plus scores of private, parochial, and charter schools. The
region attracts hundreds of thousands of students from around the
globe each year to its educational institutions, including more than
two hundred thousand college and university students to Boston, the
"Athens of America," as it is sometimes called, and Cambridge alone.[2]

---

1. Oliver Wendell Holmes, "The Autocrat of the Breakfast-Table," published first
   in the April 1858 issue of the *Atlantic Monthly*, and subsequently as *The Autocrat
   of the Breakfast-Table* (Boston: Phillips, Sampson and Co., 1861), chapter six.
   The actual quotation reads: "Boston State House is the hub of the solar system.
   You couldn't pry that out of a Boston man, if you had the tire of all creation
   straightened out for a crowbar." The phrase was later shortened to "the hub
   of the universe" or simply to "the hub." While there have been a number of
   depictions of "the hub," the best known bronze marker can be found at the
   corner of Washington and Summer streets in downtown Boston.
2. For introductions to American educational history, see Samuel Eliot
   Morison, *The Intellectual Life of Colonial New England* (Ithaca, NY:

Boston's passion for education, of course, began with its first English settlers. "Puritanism," as historian Samuel Eliot Morison reminds us, "stimulated an interest in the classics, belles lettres, poetry, and scientific research. Neither pioneer hardships nor other restrictions," he observed, "were ever so great as to prevent the burgeoning of a genuine intellectual life in that series of little beachheads on the edge of the wilderness, which was seventeenth-century New England."[3]

Originally founded in 1630, the Massachusetts Bay Colony had by 1635 established the Boston Latin School (America's oldest public school) and by 1636 it had founded Harvard College (America's oldest college).[4] Then in a series of legislative acts in 1642, 1647, and 1648, the most famous of which was known as the *Old Deluder Satan Law* of 1647, the Massachusetts General Court established the principle of free public education through its requirement that all towns of sufficient size establish elementary schools (to teach reading and writing) and grammar schools (to prepare students for college) for the training of their children.[5] "After God had carried us safe to New England, and we had builded our houses, provided necessaries for our livelihood, reared convenient places for God's worship, and settled the civil government," as *New England's First Fruits* (1643) phrases it, "one of the next things we longed for and looked after was to advance learning and perpetuate it to posterity."[6]

Cornell University Press, 1970); Bernard Bailyn, *Education in the Forming of American Society* (New York: Vintage Books, 1960); James Axtell, *The School upon a Hill* (New Haven: Yale University Press, 1974); and David Nasaw, *Schooled to Order: A Social History of Public Schooling in the United States* (New York: Oxford University Press, 1981).

3. Morison, *Intellectual Life*, 4.
4. On the founding of Harvard, see Samuel Eliot Morison, *The Founding of Harvard College* (Cambridge, MA: Harvard University Press, 1995); and Norman Fiering, *Moral Philosophy at Seventeenth-Century Harvard* (Chapel Hill: University of North Carolina Press, 1981). For the Boston Latin School see Pauline Holmes, *A Tercentenary History of the Boston Public Latin School* (Westport, CT: Greenwood Press, 1970).
5. Morison, *Intellectual Life*, 88. The law of 1647 mandated the establishment of elementary schools in all towns with fifty or more families and grammar schools in all towns with one hundred or more families.
6. Perry Miller and Thomas H. Johnson, *The Puritans: A Sourcebook of Their Writings*, 2 vols. (New York: Harper Torchbooks, 1963), 2:701. The text of

Education Begins in the Home

Puritan parents, as Edmund Morgan has observed, were responsible for their children's "souls as well as their bodies." To care
only for "their material welfare without attention to their spiritual
needs," was to look after the shoe while neglecting the foot. "If your
main concern be to get the riches of this world for your children, and
leave a belly full of this world unto them," Cotton Mather observed,
"it looks very suspiciously as if you were yourselves the people of
this world, whose portion is only in this life." Consequently, in an
effort to ensure that parents fulfilled their educational duties, the
General Court passed legislation requiring heads of households "to
teach their children and apprentices to read," to be familiar with
the laws of the commonwealth, and "to learn some short orthodox
catechism." Failure to do so, the law stipulated, would bring a penalty of "twenty shillings for each neglect therein." The purpose of
the legislation was clear: the Puritans understood that education
was not simply "a polite accomplishment" or "a means of advancing material welfare"; rather "salvation was impossible without it."
Throughout the seventeenth century, they retained the "sublime
confidence that man's chief enemy was ignorance, especially ignorance of the Scriptures." Indeed, as Increase Mather phrased it,
"Ignorance is the Mother (not of devotion but) of HERESY."[7]

"The Puritan theory of education was a wonderfully unified and
integrated whole," combining the study of Scripture with a study of
the natural world, a study of theology with a knowledge of the classics, and an examination of special revelation without neglecting
the arts and sciences. "All streams do naturally lead down to the
ocean," as Samuel Willard phrased it, "and all divine truths do as
certainly carry us home to God himself, who is the essential truth.
As truth comes from God, so it leads back to God."[8]

New England's First Fruits can also be found in Morison, appendix D, *The
Founding of Harvard College*, 419–51.

7. The quotations are taken from Edmund S. Morgan, *The Puritan Family* (New
   York: Harper & Row, 1966), 87–88. See also Levin L. Schucking, *The Puritan Family: A Social Study from the Literary Sources* (New York: Schocken Books, 1970).
8. Samuel Willard quoted in Leland Ryken, *Worldly Saints: The Puritans as
   They Really Were* (Grand Rapids: Zondervan, 1986), 170–71.

Park Street Church

As the inheritors of the Puritan mantle, therefore, it is hardly surprising that the founders of Park Street Church were also deeply committed to the life of the mind. After all, as we have seen, every one of Park Street's first four ministers became college presidents when their tenure in Boston had been completed—Edward Griffin at Williams, Sereno Dwight at Hamilton, Edward Beecher at Illinois, and Joel Linsley at Marietta.[9] Of even greater significance, perhaps, has been Park Street's close relationship with the hundreds of educational institutions that have become part of the Boston community.

In virtually every era of Park Street's history, literally thousands of faculty members and students have found their way to Park Street Church while they are teaching or pursuing their elementary, secondary, undergraduate, or graduate studies in one of Boston's educational institutions. A recent survey, for example, confirmed that fully 40 percent of those currently attending Park Street Church are students—including, of course, hundreds of international students representing more than fifty different nations from around the world.[10] And many of the teachers and students who have made their way to Boston have come to the region specifically to study or teach at one of New England's many schools or because of Boston's reputation as the Athens of America.

The City Missionary Society of Boston

Park Street's first major educational project, reflecting its commitment to missionary outreach, was its role in the establishment of the City Missionary Society of Boston. As the second oldest family welfare

9. The close ties with educational institutions has continued throughout Park Street's history as illustrated by Harold John Ockenga who also served as president of Gordon College, Gordon-Conwell Theological Seminary, and Fuller Theological Seminary; Paul Toms, who served for many years on the Board of Trustees of Gordon-Conwell Theological Seminary; and Gordon Hugenberger, who has been part of the teaching faculty at Gordon-Conwell Theological Seminary since 1974.
10. The survey was conducted on April 8, 2001, and its findings were reported in Gordon P. Hugenberger, "A Self-Portrait," *Park Street Church 2001 Annual Report*, Park Street Church archives.

agency in the nation, the City Missionary Society grew "directly from the concern of two Boston Congregational Churches [Old South and Park Street churches] for the well-being of the disadvantaged city dweller."[11] Long before it became popular to think of Boston as a potential mission field, Park Street's leaders—many of whom had also been actively involved in the establishment of the American Board of Commissioners for Foreign Missions—began to look for ways in which they could meet the growing needs of their own city.

The focus of the society during those early years was upon the "poor and needy," including "the lives of sailors, immigrants, foreign language groups, tenement dwellers, landlords, children, parents, widows and factory workers."[12] With the rapid growth of the city, its population nearly doubling during the last quarter of the eighteenth century, had come prosperity for some but increasing poverty and trouble for many others. Encouraged by Ward Stafford, a missionary who had been working with the poor children of New York City, a group of evangelical Trinitarians from Old South and Park Street, including William Thurston, Henry Homes, and Joshua Huntington, met together to discuss what might be done for the poor and needy of Boston. By visiting "some five hundred homes," they learned to their great dismay that many of the city's families neither owned a Bible nor knew anything about the Christian faith. Equally disturbing was their discovery that many of Boston's children "had never been to school and were completely illiterate."[13] As a result, the leaders, composed primarily of Christian laypeople, identified two primary tasks in which they believed the society should be engaged: welfare and education. "A great wave of social sentiment," as one observer phrased it, "poured itself out from among all who had the faculty of large and disinterested thinking."[14]

---

11. Frederick M. Meek, foreword to *A Light to the City: 150 Years of the City Missionary Society of Boston, 1816–1966*, by J. Leslie Dunstan (Boston: Beacon Press, 1966), vi.

12. Ibid., v.

13. Dunstan, *A Light to the City*, 15.

14. James Truslow Adams, *New England in the Republic* (Boston: Little, Brown & Co., 1926), 353.

So it was, as an outgrowth of those conversations, that the City Missionary Society of Boston was officially launched on October 9, 1816. Its programmatic goals, reflecting the breadth of the founders' vision, included the establishment of Sabbath schools to provide religious instruction, the building of a chapel and the provision of a pastor to minister to sailors and seamen, the launching of "charity schools" (to provide basic training in reading and writing), and the provision of means for unchurched families (unable to pay the usual pew rents) to attend worship. On May 11, 1817, the society opened its first Sabbath school for 336 children, with some of the funding and personnel provided by Park Street Church. A second, for 164 students, was opened in June and two more the following year. Then, on August 9, 1818, worship for seamen and visiting sailors was conducted for the first time under the observatory on Central Wharf by William Jenks. In addition to these ministries, the society also launched several "charity schools" to teach reading and writing to those children who were either "too ignorant to be admitted to the Common Schools" or "whose parents could not pay for them to go to private schools."[15] And finally, the society launched a number of Bible studies in private homes for those families who were not able to pay the pew rents at the churches of the city. Eventually, in fact, they were able to rent an upstairs room, known as Harry's Hall, on the west side of town where services of worship were held each Sunday afternoon and on Wednesday evenings.[16]

From the City Missionary Society of Boston, either directly or indirectly, a variety of additional ministries have been established across successive years: neighborhood Sabbath schools and vacation Bible schools, classes in baby care and sewing for young mothers, the Boston branch of the YWCA, the Penitent Female Refuge to care for young women who want to leave a life of prostitution, special ministries to prisoners and hospital patients, legal assistance

---

15. For a different perspective on the development of "common" and "charity" schools, see Nasaw, *Schooled to Order*, 18–84.

16. I am indebted to Dunstan, *A Light to the City*, 23–36, for his helpful discussion of these developments.

for those who are unable to afford it, and camping programs for urban youth, to name but a few.[17] From the vision of a small handful of Old South and Park Street members, seeking to apply the missionary mandate at home as well as abroad, an organization emerged that has served for many years as the conscience of a city.

The Tradition Continues

As remarkable as the work of the City Missionary Society has been, it has not been by any means Park Street's only educational project. In 1829, for example, the congregation launched its own Sabbath school program, establishing a tradition of Christian education that has continued to this very day. By the 1850s, furthermore, branch schools were being organized to serve the needs of children in other sections of Boston.[18] By the mid twentieth century, it was becoming apparent that increasing numbers of people, both within the church and the broader community, were biblically and theologically illiterate. Consequently, in the autumn of 1942, Harold John Ockenga of Park Street Church and Howard W. Ferrin of Providence Bible Institute decided to establish the Boston Evening School of the Bible. "It was their desire," as the opening announcement phrased the rationale, "to help Christian people in all churches, irrespective of denomination, to secure a thorough and systematic knowledge of the Bible and practical training for various kinds of Christian work." Dr. Morton C. Campbell, Professor Emeritus at the Law School of Harvard University and a member of Park Street Church, agreed to serve as dean and treasurer. And so, under the auspices of Park Street Church in cooperation with Providence Bible Institute, classes, including the study of Romans (Howard W. Ferrin), Personal Evangelism (Carlton

17. See the "History" section of the City Mission Society of Boston Web site, http://www.cmsboston.org/who_we_are/history.html (accessed October 5, 2007).
18. For a discussion of the Sunday school program and the "branch schools," see H. Crosby Englizian, *Brimstone Corner* (Chicago: Moody Press, 1968), 122–24. For a delightful introduction to the history of Sunday schools see Robert W. Lynn and Elliott Wright, *The Big Little School: 200 Years of the Sunday School*, 2nd ed. (Nashville: Abingdon, 1980).

Booth), Apostolic History (Harold J. Ockenga), and Archaeology (Terrelle B. Crum), were held each Tuesday evening from 7:00 until 9:20 PM, from November 2 through April 4. By engaging the program's six-year curriculum, the announcement promised, a student could cover "the contents of the entire Bible, the essentials of Christian doctrine, Personal Evangelism, Teacher Training and closely related fields."[19]

Boston Evening School of the Bible, date unknown. Courtesy of Park Street Church.

---

19. Brochure "Announcing the Opening of the Boston School of the Bible, November 2, 1943, Classes every Tuesday, 7–9:20 PM," Park Street Church archives.

The Boston Evening School attracted hundreds of students. In addition to providing a basic theological education for those who attended, it also helped to address another need as well. "The layman is playing an increasingly important role in the life of our churches," the school's leaders were convinced, and they need training if they are to fulfill these responsibilities effectively. Not only is the pastor "dangerously overburdened," they noted, but ministers are also "rarely equipped" to provide the full range of training that is needed for the work of the church. A better trained laity, therefore, will enable pastors to do their work more efficiently. "Hosts of men and women who are clearly not called of God into what we term 'full time ministry' would be more ready to give their services if they had the confidence induced by training." This, therefore, "is the *raison d'etre* of the Boston Bible School. Whatever developments the future may hold, it is expected that lay training will always loom large in the programme."[20]

While the Boston School of the Bible (and its successor the Boston Center for Christian Studies) are no longer identifiable programs within the life of the church, the goals they were seeking to achieve have been continued by a host of other organizations. Gordon-Conwell Theological Seminary's Center for Urban Ministerial Education (CUME); the Lexington Christian Academy; the Alpha program; Families Together; Small Group Ministry; the Bolivia, Czech, and Ukraine Partnerships; Café; FOCUS; Alive in Christ; Cityworks; CrossWalk; the Woman's Benevolent Society; Marketplace; Missions Festival; the ESL program; radio and internet ministries; Family Ministries; PSC Connect; the Graduate Student Ministry; Youth Ministries; Park Street Women; Stewardship; Park Street Union; Soli Deo Gloria; Children's Ministries; Christian Formation; Park Street Medical; and a host of other programs are addressing the perennial need for Christian education, training, and service within the church and community.

20. J. C. Macaulay, "Boston Bible School: Philosophy," May 10, 1966, Park Street Church archives. This four-page, typed document describes the organization's philosophy, objectives, organization, curriculum, faculty, and promotion.

Park Street School, Park Street Kids, and Boston Trinity Academy

One of Park Street's most ambitious educational projects is Park Street School, an elementary school for children from kindergarten through grade six that opened its doors in the fall of 2003. An outgrowth of Park Street Kids, a prekindergarten nursery school, the Park Street School seeks to provide greater-Boston area children "with a private education built on the foundation of a biblical Christian worldview" through promoting "high academic achievement" and striving "to nurture the growth of the whole child, intellectually, socially, emotionally, physically, and spiritually."[21]

The need for "a rigorous college preparatory school accessible to students from all neighborhoods, ethnicities, and socioeconomic backgrounds," as its mission statement expresses it, led to the establishment of Boston Trinity Academy in 2002. Located on a five-acre campus in the Hyde Park section of Boston, the school seeks to "inspire young people to set the highest standards, gain wisdom and live a life of faith" and challenges its students to foster academic excellence, intellectual curiosity, and deep Christian faith.

Theological Education

Park Street Church and Andover Theological Seminary, as we have seen, grew up as institutional siblings: established by the same parents, at approximately the same time and for precisely the same reasons. The early leaders of these two institutions raised a standard for Trinitarian orthodoxy in the midst of the success of Unitarianism in Boston and throughout the New England region. From the very beginning the leaders of Park Street Church—inspired by pastors like Edward Griffin who not only taught at Andover but also preached at Park Street—have taken a special interest in theological education.[22]

---

21. Park Street School, "Mission Statement," copy available on the Park Street Church Web site or in the Park Street archives.
22. For an introduction to the history and practice of theological education, see Heather F. Day, *Protestant Theological Education in America: A Bibliography*

"American graduate theological education, in its modern form," as William C. Ringenberg has suggested, "emerged in the early nineteenth century" with the first major theological seminary founded at Andover, Massachusetts in 1808.[23] Prior to the establishment of Andover Theological Seminary and the nearly 250 accredited theological schools that followed in its wake, ministers normally took one of two paths in their theological training. After graduating from college or university, they either continued for a year or two of additional specialized studies at the college (normally under the guidance of the president) or they became an apprentice to an established pastor. In both cases, they received hands-on mentoring by seasoned veterans in the practice of ministry—observing how they went about their duties, often using their personal libraries, and learning how to do ministry by actually doing it.

Andover Theological Seminary, in establishing the first three-year residential training center for pastors, established an entirely new way of preparing individuals for ministry. Consequently, as a recent Carnegie Foundation study has suggested, "Andover Theological Seminary was a unique institution in American higher education in three important ways": (1) as "the first free-standing graduate school in the nation, free of state finances or university resources"; (2) as the first institution to effectively unite "traditional Calvinists such as Stuart Moses, who became the first biblical professor, and New Divinity clergy such as Leonard Woods, who became the first president," in the common cause against the perceived Unitarian threat; and (3) as the first school to be "established as a post-collegiate, graduate-level program

(Metuchen, NJ: Scarecrow Press, 1985); Charles R. Foster et al., *Educating Clergy: Teaching Practices and Pastoral Imagination* (San Francisco: Jossey-Bass, 2006); Conrad Cherry, *Hurrying Toward Zion: Universities, Divinity Schools and American Protestantism* (Bloomington: Indiana University Press, 1995); and Glenn T. Miller, *Piety and Intellect: The Aims and Purposes of Ante-Bellum Theological Education* (Atlanta: Scholars Press, 1990).

23. See William C. Ringenberg, "Protestant Theological Education," in Daniel G. Reid et al., *Dictionary of Christianity in America* (Downers Grove, IL: InterVarsity Press, 1990), 378–80; and idem, *The Christian College: A History of Protestant Higher Education*, 2nd ed. (Grand Rapids: Baker, 2006).

that organized modern scholarship around professional service to society."[24]

Following Andover's lead, other seminaries were soon established, including Princeton (1812), Bangor (1814), Auburn (1818), Harvard (1819), Yale (1822), Protestant Episcopal (1823), Union of Virginia (1824), Lancaster (1825), Lutheran (1826), and Newton (1825). By 1860 there were sixty seminaries preparing about two thousand students for ministry.[25] By the mid nineteenth century, with the exception of those denominations that did not believe such specialized training was necessary for the practice of ministry, the Andover model had become the established standard for theological training. Viewed in retrospect, most would likely agree that it has served the needs of the church remarkably well. In at least one respect, however, the model tended to foster a *professional* understanding of Christian ministry and to obscure the historic principle of the *priesthood of all believers*. Not until the last half of the twentieth century, in fact, have theological seminaries begun to embrace the ancient understanding of the church as the body of Christ.

The earliest Christian communities, drawing upon the apostle Paul's powerful image, seemed to view every member as important and integral to corporate life and ministry. Some, of course, were set aside to be leaders while others labored in less visible tasks. Whatever the particular function, however, all were to live their lives and do their work to the glory of God and in service to others. We should all be "ready to seek the common good in preference to our own," wrote Clement of Rome in the late first century,[26] for "the head cannot get along without the feet. Nor, similarly, can the feet get along without the head. 'The tiniest parts of our body are essential to it, and are valuable to the total body,' [so] each must be subject to his neighbor, according to his special gifts."[27]

24. Foster, *Educating Clergy*, 194–95.
25. Ringenberg, "Protestant Theological Education," 379.
26. Cyril C. Richardson, *Early Christian Fathers* (Philadelphia: Westminster Press, 1953), 66.
27. Ibid., 61.

"Practice husbandry . . . if you are a husbandman," wrote Clement of Alexandria in the second century, "but while you till your fields, know God. Sail the sea, you who are devoted to navigation, yet call the whilst on the heavenly Pilot."[28] "Christians cannot be distinguished from the rest of the human race by country or language or customs," wrote the author of the early third-century *Letter to Diognetus.* "They do not live in cities of their own, they do not use a peculiar form of speech, they do not follow an eccentric manner of life," but rather they "follow the customs of the country in clothing and food and other matters of daily living. . . . They marry, like everyone else, and they beget children, but they do not cast out their offspring. They share their board with each other, but not their marriage bed. It is true that they are 'in the flesh,' but they do not live 'according to the flesh.' They busy themselves on earth, but their citizenship is in heaven. They obey the established laws, but in their own lives they go far beyond what the laws require." Moreover, they do these things for the glory of God and to contribute to the common good.[29]

The relatively fluid structures of the earliest communities quickly gave way to increasingly rigid categories. Patterned largely on familiar Jewish and Roman structures, the threefold organization of church officers (bishops, presbyters, and deacons) quickly established itself in many sections of the church. Furthermore, the division within the body between ordained clergy and nonordained laity began to show itself from the brief hints of the first century to the full-blown structures of the third and fourth. By the time of the *Constitutions of the Holy Apostles,* "clergy" and "laity" each had its own separate chapter and set of instructions. The medieval church, as Alister McGrath has reminded us, came to recognize "a fundamental distinction between the 'spiritual estate' (that is, the clergy, whether they were priests, bishops, or popes) and the 'temporal

---

28. W. R. Forrester, *Christian Vocation* (New York: Charles Scribner's Sons, 1953), 47.
29. Richardson, *Early Christian Fathers,* 216–17. See also Leland Ryken, *Work and Leisure in Christian Perspective* (Portland, OR: Multnomah Press, 1987), esp. 64–65.

estate' (that is, everyone else)."[30] There are "two ways of life" for those of us who are in the church, wrote Eusebius of Caesarea in the fourth century. "The one . . . devotes itself to the service of God alone" while "the other, more humble" and "more human," permits farming, trade, and "other more secular interests." The first is "the perfect form of the Christian life," while the other represents "a kind of secondary grade of piety."[31]

Not until the sixteenth century with the arrival of Protestant Reformers such as Martin Luther and John Calvin, was the division between sacred and secular seriously challenged.[32] Martin Luther, in his *Open Letter to the Christian Nobility* (1520) argued that "there is really no true, basic difference between laymen and priests, princes and bishops, between religious and secular, except for the sake of office and work, but not for the sake of status. They are all of the spiritual estate, all are truly priests, bishops, and popes. But they do not all have the same work to do. Just as all priests and monks do not have the same work." Consequently, "those who are now called 'spiritual,' that is, priests, bishops, or popes, are neither different from other Christians nor superior to them, except that they are charged with the administration of the word of God and the sacraments, which is their work and office." Therefore, "a cobbler, a smith, a peasant—each has the work and office of his trade, and yet they are all alike consecrated priests and bishops."[33] For Luther and Calvin alike, there was simply "no place in Christianity for any notion of a professional class within the church that is in a closer spiritual relationship to God than their fellows."[34]

At the heart of the Reformers' understanding of Christian

30. Alister McGrath, *Spirituality in an Age of Change: Rediscovering the Spirit of the Reformers* (Grand Rapids: Zondervan, 1994), 35.
31. Forrester, *Christian Vocation*, 35–36.
32. See, e.g., Gustaf Wingren, *Luther on Vocation* (Philadelphia: Muhlenberg Press, 1957); and John Calvin, *Institutes of the Christian Religion*, The Library of Christian Classics, ed. John T. McNeill (Philadelphia: Westminster Press, 1960), 2:1055–56.
33. Martin Luther, "To the Christian Nobility of the German Nation," in Helmut T. Lehmann, ed., *Three Treatises* (Philadelphia: Fortress Press, 1970), 14–15.
34. McGrath, *Spirituality in an Age of Change*, 35.

calling and vocation were five foundational principles: (1) It is God who does the calling; (2) God's call comes first as a gracious invitation to salvation; (3) God calls each Christian into that vocation for which he or she has been appropriately gifted by the Holy Spirit; (4) God's call must be grounded and nourished in the study of Scripture; and (5) God's call has two unchanging goals—to bring glory to God and to serve the common good. No community emphasized these principles more regularly than did the Puritans. "Faith," wrote John Cotton, one of Boston's first pastors, "is ready to embrace any homely service" if it is truly God's calling. For it is "in the shop," wrote Richard Steele, that one can "most confidently expect the presence and blessing of God." Every Christian, wrote Cotton Mather, "should have a calling"—some "special business"— through which "he may glorify God." Therefore, concluded John Cotton, we should "serve God in [our] calling[s], and do it with cheerfulness, and faithfulness, and an heavenly mind."[35]

Given this strong sense of calling and vocation among the Puritans who settled Boston in 1630, how are we to explain Robert Bellah's oft-quoted conclusion, in his book *Habits of the Heart,* that religion in America today "is as private and diverse as New England colonial religion was public and unified"?[36] What happened along the way to cause the church to forget the principles of a biblically based and God-centered community that helped to give substance and shape to the American project? The answers to these questions are, of course, complex and controversial. Among them, however, must surely be the enormous impact of the Enlightenment (with its shift from an emphasis on the glory of God to the glorification of the self), the rise of individualism (with its move from community to privatization), the coming of the Industrial Revolution (with its substitution of the gospel of wealth for the common good), and the rise of the university (with its systematic replacement of a Christian worldview with more secularized and sometimes clearly postmodern forms of pluralism). Whatever the reasons for the

35. Cotton, Steele, and Mather quoted in Ryken, *Worldly Saints,* 23–36.
36. Robert N. Bellah, *Habits of the Heart: Individualism and Commitment in American Life* (Berkeley: University of California Press, 1985), 220.

shift, it touched hundreds of congregations and scores of theological seminaries.

One of the most interesting developments in Park Street's recent history, prompted perhaps by such important initiatives as the establishment of the Boston School of the Bible and the launching of Marketplace Ministries, has been the congregation's recovery of the historic principle of the priesthood of all believers, the conviction that all genuine followers of Christ are called into ministry and are equipped by the Holy Spirit to perform that ministry. What seems to be happening, as a result, is the opening of a whole new era of expansion for Park Street Church. In recent years this has been reflected in the remarkable growth in church membership and through the establishment of new initiatives such as Park Street Kids, the Park Street School, and the Boston Trinity Academy. Harold John Ockenga, Park Street's twelfth pastor, had often prayed for a new reformation to call the church back once again to trust in God and obedience to His Word. Such a reformation, as Luther, Calvin, and the Puritans would remind us, must also involve a recovery of the importance of Christian vocation— freeing us from the tyranny of selfishness and encouraging the believing community once again to view all of its activities in light of God's glory and the common good. It is perhaps "unlikely that more than a minority will ever treat the choice of a life-work on this high level of consecration," observed W. R. Forrester, but "even if only a minority do so, they may create such a pattern of behaviour that others in their multitude may come to share in some sense the experience of living within a providential order, and so escape the cosmic loneliness of lost souls without roots in tradition or fruits in purposeful lives." The church has a duty "to present the Christian faith in market-place and school that even when the response of full belief and commitment in discipleship does not follow, recognition of the Christian values may be inculcated and Christian patterns of life be built up."[37]

---

37. Forrester, *Christian Vocation*, 214.

Colleges and Universities

In addition to its close ties with theological education, the linkages between Park Street Church and Boston's colleges and universities have also been remarkably strong. These too, as with the seminaries, are an outgrowth of New England's unique history. "Determined to establish a new Cambridge as well as a New England," as Morison phrased it in *The Founding of Harvard College*, the Puritans readily adopted the "seven Liberal Arts" that their European counterparts had been studying since the fifth century: the *Trivium* (Grammar, Rhetoric, and Logic) and the *Quadrivium* (Music, Arithmetic, Geometry, and Astronomy). To these studies, as one might expect, they added the unique Puritan flavor of Emmanuel College (Cambridge) where Harvard's namesake, John Harvard, and some thirty-five of New England's first generation of ministers and political leaders had been trained. Only six years after arriving in the New World, a community of less than ten thousand people had somehow managed to plant a college. "No similar achievement," Morison observed, "can be found in the history of modern colonization."[38]

For the Puritan, as Ryken has noted, the "primary goal" for all education was "Christian nurture and growth."[39] "Let every Student be plainly instructed, and earnestly pressed to consider well," as the author of *New England's First Fruits* described the rules and precepts observed at Harvard College during its early years, that "the main end of his life and studies is, to *know God and Jesus Christ which is eternal life*," and "therefore to lay *Christ* in the bottom, as the only foundation of all sound knowledge and Learning."[40] Therefore, the writer continued, every student "shall so exercise himself in reading the Scriptures twice a day, that he shall be ready to give such an

---

38. Morison, *The Founding of Harvard College*, 8, 148. "There are three things which above all we desire all the Fellows of this college to attend to," the Emmanuel College (Cambridge) regulations declared, namely "the worship of God, the increase of the faith, and probity of morals." Ryken, *Worldly Saints*, 161.
39. Ryken, *Worldly Saints*, 161.
40. Morison, appendix D: "New England's First Fruits," *The Founding of Harvard College*, 434.

account of his proficiency therein, both in *Theoretical* observations of the Language, and *Logic*, and in *Practical* and spiritual truths, as his Tutor shall require, according to his ability," seeing that "*the entrance of the word giveth light.*" Furthermore, students shall eschew "all profanation of God's Name, Attributes, Word, Ordinances, and times of Worship" and shall study "with good conscience, carefully to retain God, and the love of his truth in their minds, else let them know, that (notwithstanding their Learning) God may give them up to *strong delusions, and in the end to a reprobate mind.*"[41]

While many of America's colleges and universities have long since abandoned these kinds of religious requirements, it is equally true that a substantial number of the students on those campuses are either profoundly committed to the Christian faith themselves or they are open to explore how Christianity might relate to their own lives.[42]

Across the years, Park Street Church has become a spiritual oasis for students and faculty members from around the world. In more recent years, a ministry known as Real Life Boston has emerged with the mission of giving "every student in Boston the chance to hear the gospel of Jesus Christ in the most relevant way possible." Through a variety of programs—and in cooperation with a number of other campus-based ministries from InterVarsity Christian Fellowship to Campus Crusade for Christ—Real Life Boston seeks, as they like to phrase it, to introduce the "200,000 students at 47 of the top schools in the country" to Jesus Christ, the one who is the good news of the Christian gospel. By so doing, they are standing in a long and distinguished tradition that (since Park Street's founding) has been at the heart of the congregation's ministry in Boston.[43]

It is essential, Harold John Ockenga told a Park Street audience

---

41. Ibid.
42. See George M. Marsden, *The Soul of the American University: From Protestant Establishment to Established Nonbelief* (New York: Oxford University Press, 1994).
43. *Park Street Church 2007 Annual Report*, 14. Additional information on Real Life Boston can be found on the Park Street Church Web site.

in 1952, that we continue to ask questions about "the goals, the aims and purposes of education." From what foundation, he asked the congregation, does education derive its morality? "Certainly it is not from the educational method itself," he answered, for one's method is the result of one's philosophy. If that philosophy is relativistic or based simply upon human experience, for example, then such practices as "lying, murder, stealing," and the like, may well be "justifiable." If one believes that morality "is derived from a divinely revealed standard which is changeless," on the other hand, then one's understanding of right and wrong will need to be adjusted according to the teachings of that standard.

For many years, Ockenga observed, American education has sought to "make better citizens," to establish sound "habits and outlook," to make people "more successful" and to help them discover "a better life." Within the American tradition, moreover, "the moral life is expressed in righteousness, brotherhood and self-control." Individuals are "considered equal by creation, endowed with rights which cannot be curbed. Hence," he continued, "morality has been centered on such truths." But is it possible to achieve such lofty goals when "modern educators" insist on changing "the foundation of our morality"? Like it or not, Ockenga asserted, America's treasured rights "to life, liberty and the pursuit of happiness" are only possible when they are founded upon the teachings of the Bible. "Back of these teachings lay the Christian faith concerning a moral universe, revealed law, and human responsibility," and all of these are "postulated on the existence of God." Individuals were created by God as moral beings, therefore, right and wrong are "determined from theological concepts." Indeed, however we might feel about it, "the whole morality of Western civilization is a Christian morality."

"American education has been committed to this ideal throughout its history," Ockenga believed. What protections we have enjoyed from such dangers as "murder, theft, violence, libel" and the like are the direct result of "inalienable rights" conferred upon us by God. We are not protected because people find it "expedient not to murder, or to steal, or to lie." We are protected because "our laws express the will of God as revealed to us in the writings of the Hebrew-Christian tradition." Yet, Ockenga lamented, morality has been "cut loose from such grounding in divine authority, in a moral universe, in revealed law and in human responsibility." Philosophies such as "Experimentalism," "Operationalism," and "Functionalism" have replaced absolutes with relatives in morality, and "divine sanctions" with "human sanctions" in practice. As a result, Ockenga observed, "American moral life is in collapse with juvenile delinquency, with mounting crime," with "drunkenness, graft, immorality, breakdown of the family and public dishonesty." This debacle could be traced "to a defective moral education of our people. It is not enough to form habits, to declare that righteousness is its own reward, [or] to think that morality will stand of itself, Ockenga concluded. "Morality needs the ground and support of the will and law of God."[44]

One need not agree with Ockenga's conclusions to recognize the enormous importance that such a position places upon the role of education. This may be the reason, at least in part, that Ockenga so often spoke of Christ's Great Commission as including not only worldwide evangelization, humanitarian action, and the responsibility for moral reform, but also "the work of Christian education."[45] It may also explain, in part at least, why Park Street Church has remained throughout its history so clearly committed to Christian education, so deeply involved in the life of Boston's educational institutions, and so profoundly convinced that one's pursuit of the life of the mind can be an act of genuine spiritual worship.

---

44. Harold John Ockenga, "Morality in Education" (sermon, Park Street Church, October 19, 1952), 1–15, Ockenga Papers.
45. Harold John Ockenga, "The Foundations of Park Street Church" (sermon, February 22, 1959, on the occasion of the congregation's 150th anniversary), Ockenga Papers.

c h a p t e r   s i x

Reclaiming the Heritage

W ere Elias Boudinot to visit Park Street Church on the occasion of its two hundredth anniversary, rather than shortly after its birth two centuries earlier, he would discover a vibrant, growing, and exceptionally active congregation. He would observe, to his great delight, the nearly two thousand people—from many states and from more than sixty different nations around the globe—who gather for worship each week at one of Park Street's four Sunday services. He would almost certainly notice that nearly 70 percent of those in attendance are in their twenties and thirties—and, given his penchant for counting things, he would likely inquire as to how many were students (38 percent) and how many were married (36 percent). He would be interested to learn that the proportion of women to men is 60 percent to 40 percent among those in their twenties, 52 percent to 48 percent for those in their thirties, 50 percent to 50 percent for those in their forties, and 49 percent to 51 percent for all who are fifty years of age or older. He would be fascinated to learn that 61 percent of those who attend the church live within seven miles of the building and that 34 percent are also regularly involved in one or more of the small group gatherings sponsored by the church during the week. He would notice that the two Sunday evening services, largely contemporary in style and often led by Associate Minister Daniel Harrell, currently represent about 40 percent of Park Street's weekly attendance, and he would undoubtedly be intrigued to see that both traditional and contemporary worship styles are available within a single congregation. He would be surprised, I suspect, to discover that more than half of those in attendance have been part of the church for less than three years (due in large measure to the high percentage of students in the congregation); that the congregation gives 40 percent of its money to missions; and that the members of Park Street provide full support for nearly thirty of their own missionaries. And he would undoubtedly comment on the fact that "pew rents" were no longer required.[1]

Given his special interest in architecture, Boudinot would probably also want to examine the subtle changes that have been made to the building over the years as the congregation has purchased new space along Park Street and as various renovations have taken place. He would insist on riding the elevators. He would remark on the changes to "Bullfinch Row" and the Boston Common. He would undoubtedly note that while Park Street's famous steeple has remained essentially unchanged, the front entrances have been altered across the years—first to make room for the commercial shops that were rented out on the first floor during the late nineteenth and early twentieth centuries and later to accommodate the innovative Mayflower Pulpit that was added during Harold John Ockenga's pastorate.

One might suspect, however, that Boudinot's most striking discovery would have relatively little to do with changing demographics, architectural alterations, technological advances, or even the enormous growth of the city of Boston itself. Rather, one can imagine, he would be fascinated by the fact that Park Street's theological convictions and ministry goals have remained virtually unchanged since he and Edward Griffin discussed them in Andover so many

---

1. The statistical information is taken from Gordon P. Hugenberger, "A Self Portrait," *Park Street Church 2004 Annual Report*, Park Street Church archives. This summarizes a congregational survey conducted at all four services on Sunday, February 29, 2004.

Park Street Church steeple. Photo from Park Street Church Annual Report.
Courtesy of Park Street Church.

years before. While the delivery systems may have shifted with the
times, the core values that prompted Park Street's founders to plant
a church in the heart of Boston in 1809 are precisely the same values that continue to shape Park Street's life and work today: namely,
an unswerving commitment to biblical orthodoxy, to education, to

world missions, to social reform, to personal holiness, and to spiritual renewal. Park Street is widely known, of course, for the many historic events that have taken place within its walls and for the prominent leaders who have spoken from its pulpit. While these memories are a continual source of inspiration and a cause for celebration, however, Park Street's most significant legacy can be found in its two centuries of faithful ministry in the heart of Boston and the worldwide impact of its missionary vision around the world.

"As we look to the future," Harold John Ockenga reminded the congregation on the eve of its one hundred fiftieth anniversary celebrations, we must "remember that though all other things change," God remains ever the same. "Jesus Christ is the same yesterday, today and forever. Moreover," he observed, "human need and the Gospel do not change." What saved men and women, boys and girls in the year 1809 is exactly what will save them today. Therefore, if we continue to be faithful to our divine commission, God will prosper and bless us in the future just as God has blessed us in the past. Indeed, there will be "no divine blessing upon this congregation" without its continued "obedience to God." This means, Ockenga warned, that Park Street must remain "faithful to God's revealed truth versus all non-orthodox movements of today, whether liberal, neo-orthodox or Unitarian. As our forefathers raised a witness against Unitarianism, so we must fearlessly raise our witness against modern heretical movements. We may not join religiously with those who repudiate the Biblical concept of the Trinity, or the atonement, and of the way of salvation." Second, we must remain faithful to "the missionary vision," for God's blessing over these past decades has been in exact proportion to the level of our commitment to the support of missionary outreach. Third, we must remain faithful in our commitment to evangelism. By every appropriate means available to us—from Bible study groups and evangelistic campaigns to our determined stand against injustice and other social ills—we must seek "in every possible way" to bring the gospel to all. Fourth, we must remain faithful to "a program of educational activity" that can help "to infuse Christian truth into every realm of life." And finally, we must be faithful in restoring and maintaining the magnificent facilities God has provided for us in the heart of this great city. "In the last twenty years we have spent a half million dollars on this plant in restoring it and enlarging it." But "we have still greater plans for the future," and we "urge our people to build an endowment which will insure its permanence."

"Surely the lines have fallen to us in pleasant places," Ockenga observed. "We have a goodly heritage. Then let us maintain our testimony, our place of worship, our missionary vision, our evangelistic outreach, our prophetic societal preaching and our educational interests." Rather than adopting "the easy way," he suggested, "let us take a new look at this institution, its contribution to Boston, New England and the world, its history, its value in this location, its present program and work." This is no time to rest on our laurels, he urged, rather "it is time to go forward," expecting "great things from God" and attempting "great things for God."[2]

It is a rare achievement when any organization remains faithful to its founding principles for even a few generations. When it does so for more than two centuries, despite the normal vicissitudes of institutional life, shifts in leadership, and dramatic cultural changes, it is certainly deserving of special notice, even genuine celebration. While Park Street Church has had its own institutional ups and downs since its founding in 1809, to be sure, its guiding principles have remained remarkably consistent throughout its history. Even a cursory examination of Park Street's annual budget and its wide range of programs—including the Adult Education and Christian Formation programs, Alpha, Café, Cityworks, CrossWalk, Enable Boston, Faith@Work, Family Ministries, FOCUS, the Graduate Student Ministry, the Media Ministry, the Music Ministry and Sunday Night Band, Park Street Medical, Park Street Union, Park Street Women, Pastoral Care, Real Life Boston College Ministry, Small Group Ministry, Soli Deo Gloria, the Stewardship Education Ministry, Wings, the Woman's Benevolent Society, and the Youth Ministry—will reveal the congregation's continued commitment

---

2. All of the above quotations are taken from Harold John Ockenga, "Our Historical Heritage" (sermon, Park Street Church, Boston, February 2, 1969), 1–12, Ockenga Papers.

to education, evangelism, missionary outreach, social action, and personal discipleship.[3]

Friendship to International Students and Scholars Program

While all of Park Street's major ministry programs reflect the congregation's historic values, its Friendship to International Students and Scholars (FOCUS) program illustrates the congregation's commitments especially well. Designed as a friendship ministry to international guests and students, FOCUS provides a wide array of educational opportunities to international guests—from English language classes and Bible studies (in English, Chinese, French, Spanish, and Farsi) to special seminars and workshops such as "How to Survive and Thrive in a U.S. University," "Navigating the U.S. Healthcare System," "A Christian Critique of American Culture," "Culture Shock," "Introduction to Christian Beliefs," and "Four Essential Elements to Communicating Competently in English." Gatherings for "Tea" are held each Friday afternoon to provide opportunity for internationals to practice their English skills in actual conversation. In addition to their regular gatherings for prayer and fellowship, other opportunities are also provided for those who are interested: sightseeing trips, suppers in homes, special weekend conferences, and extended bus trips. The FOCUS ministry also oversees a six-room residence for internationals, the Van Baay Carriage House in Cambridge, across from the Harvard Law School. Affiliated with International Students, Inc., a nationwide Christian organization, FOCUS seeks to prepare mature Christian international students and scholars for ministry leadership in America and abroad.

With more than a half million international students currently studying in American universities, Stuart DeLorme has observed, "the fields are white unto harvest." During Joseph Sabounji's twenty-seven-year ministry at Park Street, DeLorme continued,

---

3. For more detailed descriptions of these programs see the *Park Street Church 2007 Annual Report*, 11–14.

"by the grace of God, many internationals"—from such places as India, China, Japan, Turkey, Saudi Arabia, and Indonesia—"were ministered to through FOCUS, for which we give God all praise and glory."[4] Much remains to be done, of course. But as Hugenberger likes to remind the Park Street congregation, borrowing the words of John Haggai, the founder and president of the Haggai Institute for Advanced Leadership Training, we should "attempt something so great for God that it's doomed to failure unless God be in it." We want to be, Hugenberger often adds, "a church whose vitality and love for each other cannot be explained apart from God."[5]

Park Street's Core Staff

Helping to oversee these programs is an enormously gifted group of women and men who make up the current Park Street Church staff. As they are quick to note, however, they are simply the servants of the One who is the true Head of the church. Like John the Baptist before them, they freely confess: "I am not the Christ."[6] Who was John? "We know who he wasn't," Hugenberger responds; "He wasn't the Christ." So who was he? By his own admission, John was "a walking sign post"—a visual "advertisement for Jesus. You see him but you don't see him. You just see the arrow and you look to Christ." Or as John the Baptist himself phrased it, "You yourselves can testify that I said, 'I am not the Christ but am sent ahead of him.' The bride belongs to the bridegroom. The friend who attends the bridegroom waits and listens for him, and is full of joy when he hears the bridegroom's voice. That joy is mine, and it is now complete. He must become greater; I must become less."[7] Across two centuries of history, the leadership of Park Street—in

---

4. Stuart DeLorme has served as Minister to Internationals since 1998. His predecessor, Joseph Sabounji, served in that capacity from 1971 until 1998. E-mail, Stuart DeLorme to Garth Rosell, April 18, 2008.

5. Quotations taken from Tom Telford, *Today's All-Star Missions Churches: Strategies to Help Your Church Get into the Game* (Grand Rapids: Baker, 2001), 82–83.

6. See Gordon Hugenberger, "I Am Not the Christ" (sermon, n.d., Park Street Church); available through Park Street's audio ministry. The sermon is based on John 1:19–28.

7. John 3:28–30.

Park Street Church staff, 2008. Courtesy of Park Street Church.

its best moments—has known that it is not about them. Rather, it
is about the living Christ—who came to seek and to save those who
are lost.

The Park Street Pulpit

Since its founding in 1809, the ministry of Park Street Church
has found its center in the pulpit and the Word. While a wide array
of ministries have certainly enlarged and deepened Park Street's
influence in Boston and around the world, it has been the faithful
exposition of the Bible that has remained the heart and soul of congregational life. For those who might wonder how any church can
remain true to its founding principles across so many years, Park
Street's answer has consistently remained clear and direct: through
the faithful preaching of God's Word and through the faithful
application of that Word by God's people.[8]

"You may be new to Park Street Church," Hugenberger observed
during the congregation's sixty-eighth missions conference.
Indeed, you may be surprised to see our display of flags from many
nations around the world. While many American churches have
become "inwardly focused," Park Street has always been "a church
with a global vision." When you become involved with this congregation, "you suddenly fall in love with the world." Part of the
reason, of course, "is that our worshippers come from more than
sixty nations." When you are surrounded "with human beings,
dear women and men with their children, who have come from
areas of the world where even mission activities would be out-
lawed," Hugenberger concluded, it is difficult "to have a parochial
concern."[9]

For the past two centuries, in times of abundance and in seasons of scarcity, members of Park Street Church have been falling

---

8. See John Calvin, *Institutes of the Christian Religion*, in The Library of
   Christian Classics, 2 vols., ed. John T. McNeill (Philadelphia: Westminster
   Press, 1960), 2:1023. "Wherever we see the Word of God purely preached
   and heard, and the sacraments administered according to Christ's institution, there, it is not to be doubted, a church of God exists."
9. Gordon Hugenberger, "Following Jesus in a Not-So-Flat World" (sermon, Park Street Church, November 11, 2007).

in love with that world and seeking, by word and deed, to serve its nearly six and a half billion inhabitants in the name of their Master, Jesus Christ. They have not always been obedient to the biblical mandates, to be sure, but in their best moments they have sought to love God with all their heart, soul, mind, and strength and to love their neighbor as they love themselves. They have not always been successful, as contemporary standards often judge success, yet God has been pleased to dwell in their midst. And while they have not always lived up to the historic values to which they claim to be committed, by God's grace those values have never been totally abandoned. Indeed, they remain the foundation on which each successive generation has continued to build.

There is reason to hope that Park Street's best years have yet to be experienced. The past, of course, can instruct and inspire—but much remains to be accomplished. For the God who called and empowered the congregation's pioneers is the same God who continues to call and empower our generation to serve a needy world with intelligence, compassion, commitment, and joy. "He who began a good work in you," the great missionary apostle reminds us, "will carry it on to completion until the day of Christ Jesus."[10] Thanks be to God.

Soli Deo Gloria

---

10. Philippians 1:6.

Epilogue

Since its founding in 1630, Boston has been a magnet for visitors from virtually every part of the world. Drawn by the region's scenic beauty, fascinating history, and quaint charm, many of these guests have also discovered New England's rich spiritual heritage. For the thousands who travel Boston's famous Freedom Trail, the 2.5-mile redbrick walking tour of sixteen of the city's most important historic sites, a visit to Park Street Church (the third stop on the tour) has become a kind of spiritual oasis.

Park Street Church is quite properly celebrated for its illustrious history and for the many notable events that have taken place within its walls—from the storage of gunpowder in its basement during the War of 1812 to the first singing of "America." Of even greater significance, however, has been Park Street's remarkable ministry to those who for two centuries have gathered there to worship God, to study His Word, and to find forgiveness for their sins, and have then scattered to feed the hungry, care for the needy, stand for justice, and spread the glorious gospel throughout the world. Park Street Church is far more than a historic monument with a magnificent steeple. It is a living community of sinners who are being transformed by God's amazing grace and who are seeking to live their lives in faithful obedience to the Holy Scriptures.

It is this larger story, as the congregation gathers to celebrate two hundred years of history, that I was commissioned to write and that I have sought to tell throughout the pages of this book.

All historians, of course, are aware of how dependent they are on those who have gone before—that they stand, to borrow the familiar phrase, on the shoulders of giants. Although forty years have passed since H. Crosby Englizian's excellent history was first published, *Brimstone Corner: Park Street Church, Boston* remains the starting point for any serious study of the congregation's history. The foundation of Englizian's work, however, and of this little volume as well, are the extensive records of the congregation that are housed in the archives of Park Street Church (known affectionately as "The Vault"), in the Harold John Ockenga Papers housed at Gordon-Conwell Theological Seminary, at the Congregational Library on Beacon Street, and in the holdings of various libraries and archives throughout the region. Included in these collections, of course, are hundreds of sermons and letters, minutes of committee and congregational meetings, photographs and drawings, newspaper articles, publications by Park Street's pastors, books published in connection with the congregation's various anniversaries, and more general scholarly studies of the region and its institutions. Many of these, as the reader will discover, are identified in the footnotes and the bibliography.

In addition to these archival and library resources, this project has been greatly enriched by many within the Park Street community who have either responded to my questions, provided perspective on aspects of the congregation's history, helped me to locate materials, or served as readers for various manuscript drafts. I am especially grateful to Gordon Hugenberger, my pastor and treasured friend. Not only did he read and respond to several drafts of the manuscript, but the conversations we shared in his office or over lunch at the Parker House were of enormous help to me in providing perspective on Park Street's life and ministry.

I also want to thank the faculty, administration, and Board of Trustees of Gordon-Conwell Theological Seminary for their support and encouragement throughout the project, and to express my deep appreciation to friends like John Chung, Stuart DeLorme, Matthew Erickson, Muriel Clement, Ken Swetland, Ron Barndt, Anne Montague, David Horn, Bethany Sayles Yu, Joshua Kercsmer, Jonathan Duncan, Charles Woodward, Mindelynn Young, Benjamin Bythewood, Bob McKenney, Chris Gilbert, and the entire editorial staff at Kregel Publications, including Jim Weaver, Steve Barclift, Miranda Gardner, Wendy Widder, and Dawn Anderson for their help in moving the book toward publication.

My deepest gratitude, however, is reserved for my wife. Not only did Jane read each of the chapters as they were completed (usually more than once) but she also took time to discuss them with me. Of all the joys I experienced in exploring the history of Boston's historic Park Street Church, these conversations will remain my most treasured memory.

Garth M. Rosell

Selected Bibliography

Adams, James Truslow. *New England in the Republic*. Boston: Little, Brown & Co., 1926.

Ahlstrom, Sidney E., ed. *An American Reformation: A Documentary History of Unitarian Christianity*. Middletown, CT: Wesleyan University Press, 1985.

Akers, Charles W. *Called unto Liberty: A Life of Jonathan Mayhew, 1720–1766*. Cambridge, MA: Harvard University Press, 1964.

American Board of Commissioners for Foreign Missions. *View of the Missions of the American Board of Commissioners for Foreign Missions*. Boston: Crocker & Brewster, 1823.

Anderson, Courtney. *To the Golden Shore: The Life of Adoniram Judson*. Valley Forge, PA: Judson Press, 1987.

Augustine of Hippo. *The Enchiridion on Faith, Hope, and Love*. Translated by John E. Rotelle. New York: New City Press, 1999.

Axtell, James. *The School upon a Hill*. New Haven: Yale University Press, 1974.

Bacon, Edwin M. *King's Dictionary of Boston*. Cambridge, MA: King, 1883.

Bailyn, Bernard. *Education in the Forming of American Society*. New York: Vintage Books, 1960.

Baltzell, E. Digby. *Puritan Boston and Quaker Philadelphia*. Boston: Beacon Press, 1982.

Bardwell, Horatio. *Memoir of Gordon Hall.* New York: J. Leavitt, 1834.

Barnes, Gilbert Hobbs. *The Anti-Slavery Impulse: 1830–1844.* New York: Harcourt, Brace and World, 1964.

Beaver, R. Pearce. *All Loves Excelling: American Protestant Women and World Missions.* Eugene, OR: Wipf & Stock, 1998.

Beecher, Lyman. *The Bible a Code of Laws, a sermon delivered in Park Street Church, Boston, September 3, 1817 . . .* Andover, MA: Flagg & Gould, 1818.

Bellah, Robert N. *Habits of the Heart: Individualism and Commitment in American Life.* Berkeley: University of California Press, 1985.

Belmonte, Kevin. *Hero for Humanity: A Biography of William Wilberforce.* Colorado Springs, CO: NavPress, 2002.

Bendroth, Margaret Lamberts. *Fundamentalists in the City: Conflict and Division in Boston's Churches, 1885–1950.* New York: Oxford University Press, 2005.

Boyd, George. *Elias Boudinot: Patriot and Statesman, 1740–1825.* Westwood, CT: Greenwood Publications, 1969.

Broyles, Michael, ed. *Yankee Musician in Europe: The 1837 Journals of Lowell Mason.* Rochester, NY: University of Rochester Press, 1996.

Burin, Eric. *Slavery and the Peculiar Solution: A History of the American Colonization Society.* Gainesville: University of Florida Press, 2005.

Burnaby, John, ed. *Augustine: Later Works.* Philadelphia: Westminster Press, 1955.

Cairns, Earle E. *An Endless Line of Splendor: Revivals and Their Leaders from the Great Awakening to the Present.* Wheaton, IL: Tyndale House, 1986.

Calvin, John. *Institutes of the Christian Religion.* Edited by John T. McNeill. 2 vols. The Library of Christian Classics. Philadelphia: Westminster Press, 1960.

Campbell, Robert, and Peter Vanderwarker. *Cityscapes of Boston: An American City Through Time.* Boston: Houghton Mifflin, 1992.

Carey, William. *An Enquiry into the Obligations of Christians to Use Means for the Conversion of the Heathens.* Dallas: Criswell Publications, 1988.

Carpenter, Joel A. *Revive Us Again: The Reawakening of American Fundamentalism.* New York: Oxford University Press, 1997.

Chaney, Charles L. *The Birth of Missions in America*. South Pasadena, CA: Carey Library, 1976.

Cherry, Conrad. *Hurrying Toward Zion: Universities, Divinity Schools and American Protestantism*. Bloomington: Indiana University Press, 1995.

Conrad, Arcturus Z. *Boston's Awakening: A Complete Account of the Great Boston Revival*. Boston: King's Business, 1909.

————. *The One Hundred and Twenty-fifth Anniversary of Park Street Congregational Church, Boston, Massachusetts*. Boston: Park Street Church of Boston, 1934.

Cross, Barbara M., ed. *The Autobiography of Lyman Beecher*. 2 vols. Cambridge, MA: Belknap Press of Harvard University Press, 1961.

Davies, Horton. *The Worship of the American Puritans*. Morgan, PA: Soli Deo Gloria Publications, 1999.

Day, Heather F. *Protestant Theological Education in America: A Bibliography*. Metuchen, NJ: Scarecrow Press, 1985.

Dayton, Donald W. *Discovering an Evangelical Heritage*. New York: Harper & Row, 1976.

Dorsett, Lyle W. *Billy Sunday and the Redemption of Urban America*. Grand Rapids: Eerdmans, 1991.

————. *A Passion for Souls: The Life of D. L. Moody*. Chicago: Moody Press, 1997.

Dunstan, J. Leslie. *A Light to the City: 150 Years of the City Missionary Society of Boston, 1816–1966*. Boston: Beacon Press, 1966.

Dwight, Timothy. *A Sermon Preached at the Opening of the Theological Institution in Andover*. Boston: Farrand, Mallory, 1808.

Edwards, Jonathan. *The Great Awakening*. Vol. 4, The Works of Jonathan Edwards. Edited by C. C. Goen. New Haven: Yale University Press, 1972.

Emerson, Ralph Waldo. *Essays*. Boston: Ticknor and Fields, 1867.

Englizian, H. Crosby. *Brimstone Corner: Park Street Church, Boston*. Chicago: Moody Press, 1968.

Fiering, Norman. *Moral Philosophy at Seventeenth-Century Harvard*. Chapel Hill: University of North Carolina Press, 1981.

Finney, Charles G. *Lectures on Revivals of Religion*. Edited by William G. McLoughlin Jr. 1835. Reprint, Cambridge, MA: Belknap Press of Harvard University Press, 1960.

Fitzmier, John R. *New England's Moral Legislator: Timothy Dwight, 1752–1817*. Bloomington: Indiana University Press, 1998.

Fletcher, Robert Samuel. *A History of Oberlin College: From Its Foundation Through the Civil War*. 2 vols. Oberlin, OH: Oberlin College, 1943.

Foote, Henry Wilder, ed. *The Cambridge Platform of 1648*. Boston: Beacon Press, 1949.

Forrester, W. R. *Christian Vocation*. New York: Charles Scribner's Sons, 1953.

Foster, Frank Hugh. *A Genetic History of the New England Theology*. New York: Russell & Russell, 1963.

Garrison, Wendell Phillips, and Francis Jackson Garrison. *William Lloyd Garrison, 1805–1879: The Story of His Life Told by His Children*. New York: Century Company, 1885.

Garrison, William Lloyd. *Thoughts on African Colonization*. Boston: Garrison & Knapp, 1832.

Gilchrist, David T. *The Growth of Seaport Cities*. Charlottesville: University of Virginia Press, 1967.

Graham, Billy. *Just As I Am: The Autobiography of Billy Graham*. San Francisco: HarperCollins Worldwide, 1997.

Greene, Lorenzo J. *The Negro in Colonial New England*. New York: Athenaeum, 1968.

Griffin, Edward D. *The Kingdom of Christ: A Missionary Sermon, Preached Before the General Assembly of the Presbyterian Church in Philadelphia, May 23, 1805*. Philadelphia: Aitken, 1805.

———. *A Series of Lectures, Delivered in Park Street Church, Boston, on Sabbath Evening*. Boston: Nathaniel Willis, 1813.

———. *A Sermon Preached Jan. 10, 1810, at the Dedication of the Church in Park Street, Boston*. Boston: Lincoln & Edmands, 1810.

Griffin, Edward M. *Old Brick: Charles Chauncy of Boston*. Minneapolis: University of Minnesota Press, 1980.

Grout, H. M., ed. *The Gospel Invitation: Sermons Related to the Boston Revival of 1877*. Boston: Lockwood, Brooks, and Company, 1877.

Hale, Abraham G. R. "Chaplain Stone and the Religious Life of the Forty-fifth Massachusetts Regiment." In *History of the Forty-fifth Regiment*. Edited by Albert W. Mann. Boston: Wallace Spooner, 1908.

Hall, Gordon, and Samuel Newell. *The Conversion of the World.* Andover, MA: Flagg & Gould, 1818.

Hambrick-Stowe, Charles E. *Charles G. Finney and the Spirit of American Evangelicalism.* Grand Rapids: Eerdmans, 1996.

———. *The Practice of Piety: Puritan Devotional Disciplines in Seventeenth-Century New England.* Chapel Hill: University of North Carolina Press, 1982.

Handlin, Oscar. *Boston's Immigrants: 1790–1865.* Cambridge, MA: Harvard University Press, 1941.

Harper, George W. *A People So Favored of God: Boston's Congregational Churches and Their Pastors, 1710–1760.* 2nd ed. Eugene, OR: Wipf & Stock Publishers, 2007.

Heimert, Alan, and Perry Miller, eds. *The Great Awakening: Documents Illustrating the Crisis and Its Consequences.* Indianapolis: Bobbs-Merrill, 1967.

Henry, Carl F. H. *The Uneasy Conscience of Modern Fundamentalism.* Grand Rapids: Eerdmans, 1947.

Henry, Stuart C. *Unvanquished Puritan: A Portrait of Lyman Beecher.* Westport, CT: Greenwood Press, 1986.

Holmes, Oliver Wendell. *The Autocrat of the Breakfast-Table.* Boston: Phillips, Sampson and Company, 1861.

Holmes, Pauline. *A Tercentenary History of the Boston Public Latin School.* Westport, CT: Greenwood Press, 1970.

Hutchison, William R. *Errand to the World: American Protestant Thought and Foreign Missions.* Chicago: University of Chicago Press, 1987.

Hynson, Leon O. *To Reform the Nation: Theological Foundations of Wesley's Ethics.* Grand Rapids: Zondervan, 1984.

Jenkins, Philip. *The Next Christendom: The Coming of Global Christianity.* New York: Oxford University Press, 2002.

Kaiser, Walter C., Jr. *Revive Us Again: Biblical Insights for Encouraging Spiritual Renewal.* Nashville: Broadman & Holman Publishers, 1999.

Kane, J. Herbert. *A Concise History of the Christian World Mission.* Grand Rapids: Baker, 1987.

Kelly, J. N. D. *Early Christian Doctrines.* Revised ed. Peabody, MA: Prince Press, 2004.

Kennedy, Lawrence W. *Planning the City upon a Hill: Boston Since 1630.* Amherst: University of Massachusetts Press, 1992.

Knowles, James D. *Memoir of Mrs. Ann H. Judson.* Boston: Lincoln & Edmands, 1831.

Krieger, Alex, and David Cobb, eds. *Mapping Boston.* Cambridge, MA: MIT Press, 2001.

Kuyper, Abraham. "Sphere Sovereignty." In *Abraham Kuyper: A Centennial Reader.* Edited by James D. Bratt. Grand Rapids: Eerdmans, 1998.

Latourette, Kenneth Scott. *A History of the Expansion of Christianity.* 7 vols. Grand Rapids: Zondervan, 1970.

Lindsell, Harold. *Park Street Prophet: The Story of Harold Ockenga.* Wheaton, IL: Van Kampen Press, 1951.

Lippy, Charles. *Seasonable Revolutionary: The Mind of Charles Chauncy.* Lanham, MD: Rowman and Littlefield, 1981.

Long, Kathryn Teresa. *The Revival of 1857–58: Interpreting an American Religious Awakening.* New York: Oxford University Press, 1998.

Lynn, Robert W., and Elliott Wright. *The Big Little School: 200 Years of the Sunday School.* 2nd ed. Nashville: Abingdon, 1980.

MacLeod, Judith. *Woman's Union Missionary Society: The Story of a Continuing Mission.* Upper Darby, PA: InterServe USA, 1999.

Magnuson, Norris. *Salvation in the Slums.* Eugene, OR: Wipf & Stock, 2005.

Marsden, George M. *Fundamentalism and American Culture: The Shaping of Twentieth-Century Evangelicalism, 1870–1925.* New York: Oxford University Press, 1980.

———. *Jonathan Edwards: A Life.* New Haven: Yale University Press, 2003.

———. *The Soul of the American University: From Protestant Establishment to Established Nonbelief.* New York: Oxford University Press, 1994.

Massachusetts Historical Society. *Letters and Documents Relating to Slavery in Massachusetts.* 5th series. Boston: Massachusetts Historical Society Collections, 1877.

Mayer, Henry. *All on Fire: William Lloyd Garrison and the Abolition of Slavery.* New York: St. Martin's Griffin, 1998.

McGrath, Alister. *Spirituality in an Age of Change: Rediscovering the Spirit of the Reformers.* Grand Rapids: Zondervan, 1994.

Mead, Sidney E. *Nathaniel William Taylor, 1786–1858: A Connecticut Liberal.* North Haven, CT: Archon Books, 1967.

Miller, Glenn T. *Piety and Intellect: The Aims and Purposes of Ante-Bellum Theological Education.* Atlanta: Scholars Press, 1990.

Miller, Perry, and Thomas H. Johnson. *The Puritans: A Sourcebook of Their Writings.* 2 vols. New York: Harper Torchbooks, 1963.

Mitchell, Rudy. *History of Revivalism in Boston.* Boston: Emmanuel Gospel Center, 2007.

Moberg, David O. *The Great Reversal: Evangelism and Social Concern.* Philadelphia and New York: J. B. Lippincott, 1972.

Moody, William R. *The Life of Dwight L. Moody.* New York: Revell, 1900.

Moore, Martin. *Boston Revival, 1842: A Brief History of the Evangelical Churches of Boston Together with a More Particular Account of the Revival of 1842.* Wheaton, IL: R. O. Roberts, 1980.

Morgan, Edmund S. *The Puritan Family.* New York: Harper & Row, 1966.

Morison, Samuel Eliot. *The Intellectual Life of Colonial New England.* Ithaca, NY: Cornell University Press, 1970.

Nasaw, David. *Schooled to Order: A Social History of Public Schooling in the United States.* New York: Oxford University Press, 1981.

Neill, Stephen, and Owen Chadwick. *A History of Christian Missions.* New York: Penguin, 1991.

Newell, Harriet. *The Life and Writings of Mrs. Harriet Newell.* Philadelphia: American Sunday School Union, 1831.

Niebuhr, H. Richard. *Christ and Culture.* Expanded ed. New York: Harper, 2001.

Noll, Mark A. *America's God: From Jonathan Edwards to Abraham Lincoln.* New York: Oxford University Press, 2005.

———. *The Civil War as a Theological Crisis.* Chapel Hill: University of North Carolina Press, 2006.

———. *The Rise of Evangelicalism: The Age of Edwards, Whitefield and the Wesleys.* Downers Grove, IL: InterVarsity Press, 2003.

Orr, J. Edwin. *Campus Aflame: A History of Evangelical Awakenings in Collegiate Communities.* Wheaton, IL: International Awakening Press, 1994.

———. *The Second Evangelical Awakening in America.* London: Marshall, Morgan & Scott, 1952.

Park Street Church. *The Articles of Faith, and the Covenant, of Park Street*

Church, Boston, with a List of the Members. Boston: T. R. Marvin, 1850.

Peabody, Andrew P. *History of the Missions of the ABCFM.* Boston: Crosby and Nichols, 1862.

Pelikan, Jaroslav. *Credo: Historical and Theological Guide to Creeds and Confessions of Faith in the Christian Tradition.* New Haven: Yale University Press, 2003.

———. *The Emergence of the Catholic Tradition (100–600).* Vol. 1 of *The Christian Tradition: A History of the Development of Doctrine.* Chicago: University of Chicago Press, 1974.

Pemberton, Carol A. *Lowell Mason: His Life and Work.* Ann Arbor, MI: UMI Research Press, 1985.

Plass, Ewald M., ed. *What Luther Says: An Anthology.* 3 vols. St. Louis, MO: Concordia Press, 1959.

Porterfield, Amanda. *Mary Lyon and the Mount Holyoke Missionaries.* New York: Oxford University Press, 1997.

Revival in Our Time: The Story of the Billy Graham Evangelistic Campaigns, Including Six of His Sermons. Wheaton, IL: Van Kampen Press, 1950.

Richardson, Cyril C. *Early Christian Fathers.* Philadelphia: Westminster Press, 1953.

Ringenberg, William C. *The Christian College: A History of Protestant Higher Education.* 2nd ed. Grand Rapids: Baker, 2006.

Robert, Dana L., *American Women in Mission: A Social History of Their Thought and Practice.* Macon, GA: Mercer University Press, 1996.

———, ed. *Gospel Bearers, Gender Barriers.* Maryknoll, NY: Orbis, 2002.

Rosell, Garth M. "America's Hour Has Struck." *Christian History and Biography,* Fall 2006, 12–19.

———, ed. *Commending the Faith: The Preaching of Dwight L. Moody* Peabody, MA: Hendrickson, 1999.

———. "A Speckled Bird: Charles G. Finney's Contribution to Higher Education." *Fides et Historia,* Summer 1993, 55–74.

———. *The Surprising Work of God: Harold John Ockenga, Billy Graham and the Rebirth of Evangelicalism.* Grand Rapids: Baker, 2008.

Rosell, Garth M., and Richard A. G. Dupuis, eds. *The Memoirs of Charles G. Finney: The Complete Restored Text.* Grand Rapids: Zondervan, 1989.

Ryken, Leland. *Work and Leisure in Christian Perspective.* Portland, OR: Multnomah Press, 1987.

———. *Worldly Saints: The Puritans as They Really Were.* Grand Rapids: Zondervan, 1986.

Schaff, Philip, and Henry Wace, eds. *A Select Library of Nicene and Post-Nicene Fathers of the Christian Church.* 2nd series. Vol. 14, *The Seven Ecumenical Councils.* Grand Rapids: Eerdmans, 1971.

Schreiner, Samuel A. *The Passionate Beechers.* Hoboken, NJ: John Wiley, 2003.

Schucking, Levin L. *The Puritan Family: A Social Study from the Literary Sources.* New York: Schocken Books, 1970.

Scovel, Carl, and Charles C. Forman. *Journey Toward Independence: King's Chapel's Transition to Unitarianism.* Boston: Skinner House Books, 1993.

Smith, Oswald J. *The Challenge of Missions.* Carlisle, PA: Paternoster, 2005.

Smith, Timothy L. *Revivalism and Social Reform: American Protestantism on the Eve of the Civil War.* Eugene, OR: Wipf & Stock, 2005.

Snyder, Stephen H. *Lyman Beecher and His Children.* Brooklyn, NY: Carlson Publishers, 1991.

Sprague, William B. *Annals of the American Pulpit.* New York: Robert Carter and Brothers, 1857.

———. *Memoir of the Rev. Edward D. Griffin, D.D.: Compiled Chiefly from His Own Writings.* New York: Taylor & Dodd, 1839.

Spring, Gardiner. *Memoir of the Rev. Samuel J. Mills.* New York: J. Seymour, 1820.

Stone, Andrew L. "War: The Romance and the Reality: A Memorial Address by Chaplain A. L. Stone." In *History of the Forty-fifth Regiment.* Edited by Albert W. Mann. Boston: Wallace Spooner, 1908.

Stout, Harry S. *The New England Soul: Preaching and Religious Culture in Colonial New England.* New York: Oxford University Press, 1986.

Sweeney, Douglas A. *The American Evangelical Story: A History of the Movement.* Grand Rapids: Baker, 2005.

———. *Nathaniel Taylor, New Haven Theology, and the Legacy of Jonathan Edwards.* New York: Oxford University Press, 2003.

Taylor, James B. *Memoir of Rev. Luther Rice.* Baltimore: Armstrong and Berry, 1841.

Telford, Tom. *Today's All-Star Missions Churches: Strategies to Help Your Church Get into the Game.* Grand Rapids: Baker, 2001.

Tennent, Timothy C. *Theology in the Context of World Christianity: How the Global Church Is Influencing the Way We Think About and Discuss Theology.* Grand Rapids: Zondervan, 2007.

Thomas, Milton Halsey, ed. *Elias Boudinot's Journey to Boston in 1809.* Princeton, NJ: Princeton University Press, 1955.

Tracy, Joseph. *The Great Awakening.* Edinburgh, U.K.: Banner of Truth, 1997.

————. *History of the American Board of Commissioners for Foreign Missions.* New York: M. W. Dodd, 1842.

Trumbull, Henry Clay. *Old Time Student Volunteers.* New York: Revell, 1902.

Tucker, Ruth A. *Guardians of the Great Commission: The Story of Women in Modern Missions.* Grand Rapids: Zondervan, 1988.

Tucker, Ruth A., and Walter Liefeld. *Daughters of the Church.* Grand Rapids: Zondervan, 1987.

Walls, Andrew F. *The Missionary Movement in Christian History.* Maryknoll, NY: Orbis, 1996.

Walls, Andrew F., and Cathy Ross, eds. *Mission in the 21st Century: Exploring the Five Marks of Global Mission.* Maryknoll, NY: Orbis, 2008.

Wesley, John. *Thoughts upon Slavery.* London: R. Hawes, 1774.

Williams, Rowan. *Arius: Heresy and Tradition.* Revised ed. Grand Rapids: Eerdmans, 2001.

Wingren, Gustaf. *Luther on Vocation.* Philadelphia: Muhlenberg Press, 1957.

Woods, Leonard. *History of Andover Theological Seminary.* Boston: J. R. Osgood, 1885.

Worcester, Samuel M. *A Memorial of the Old and New Tabernacle, Salem, Mass. 1854–1855.* Boston: Crocker & Brewster, 1855.

Wright, Conrad. *The Beginnings of Unitarianism in America.* Berkeley, CA: Starr King, 1955.

————. *The Unitarian Controversy: Essays on American Unitarian History* Boston: Skinner House Books, 1994.

Wyatt-Brown, Bertram. *Lewis Tappan and the Evangelical War Against Slavery.* Cleveland: Case Western Reserve University, 1969.

Index

Page numbers appearing in *italics* refer to photographs or figures.